THIS BOOK BELONGS TO

_____

START DATE

_____

SHE READS TRUTH

EXECUTIVE

FOUNDER/CHIEF EXECUTIVE OFFICER
Raechel Myers

CO-FOUNDER/CHIEF CONTENT OFFICER
Amanda Bible Williams

CHIEF OPERATING OFFICER
Ryan Myers

EXECUTIVE ASSISTANT
Sarah Andereck

EDITORIAL

EDITORIAL DIRECTOR
Jessica Lamb

MANAGING EDITOR
Beth Joseph, MDiv

DIGITAL MANAGING EDITOR
Oghosa Iyamu, MDiv

ASSOCIATE EDITOR
Tameshia Williams, ThM

EDITORIAL ASSISTANT
Hannah Little

EDITORIAL INTERN
Bailey Shoemaker

MARKETING

PRODUCT MARKETING MANAGER
Wesley Chandler

SOCIAL MEDIA STRATEGIST
Taylor Krupp

COMMUNITY SUPPORT SPECIALIST
Margot Williams

CREATIVE

CREATIVE DIRECTOR
Jeremy Mitchell

LEAD DESIGNER
Kelsea Allen

DESIGNERS
Abbey Benson
Davis Camp DeLisi
Annie Glover

JUNIOR DESIGNER
Lauren Haag

LOGISTICS

LOGISTICS MANAGER
Lauren Gloyne

PROJECT ASSISTANT
Mary Beth Montgomery

COMMUNITY SUPPORT

CUSTOMER SUPPORT MANAGER
Kara Hewett

CUSTOMER SUPPORT SPECIALISTS
Elise Matson
Katy McKnight

SHIPPING

FULFILLMENT LEAD
Abigail Achord

FULFILLMENT SPECIALISTS
Cait Baggerman
Noe Sanchez

SUBSCRIPTION INQUIRIES
orders@shereadstruth.com

CONTRIBUTOR

SPECIAL THANKS
Bailey Gillispie

@SHEREADSTRUTH

Download the
She Reads Truth app,
available for iOS
and Android

Subscribe to the
She Reads Truth podcast

SHEREADSTRUTH.COM

This book was printed offset in Nashville, Tennessee, on 70# Lynx Opaque. Cover is 100# Cougar Opaque with a soft touch lamination.

DO NOT FEAR

A BIBLICAL STUDY ON RESPONDING TO GOD'S FAITHFULNESS

Each command provides the means of obedience, the real solution to not only enduring but overcoming fear: the consistent character of our faithful, ever present God.

Jessica

Jessica Lamb
EDITORIAL DIRECTOR

When do you feel fear? My first pass at filling out the inventory on page 18 didn't require me to think too hard. Most of us can easily come up with a list of items in the general category of fright: cockroaches, snakes, clowns, heights, needles. I have one dear friend who grimaces at the sight of a belly button. We have a beloved coworker who is so easily startled that we keep a record of how many days it has been since her last piercing shriek.

If I sit with the question longer, deeper and quieter concerns I seldom speak out loud or write on paper begin to surface—fears that keep me awake into the early morning, or that I've learned to keep buried as I go throughout my day. I know I'm not alone in this. Some fears are driven by present circumstances and needs. Others are rooted in the wounds of my past, pain I've caused myself and others or from trauma at the hands of another. Then there are my insecurities and doubts about the world, myself, and my relationships. The longer I reflect, the more I have to write down.

Yet the Bible repeatedly tells us, in stories and straightforward commands: "Do not fear." Frankly, this command can feel impossible, or even foolish, given the realities of the world we live in. But as we discovered while creating this reading plan, these scriptures are not a command to grit our teeth, muster up internal resolve, and get over our long lists. Each command also provides the means of obedience, the real solution to not only enduring but overcoming fear: the consistent character of our faithful, ever present God.

Instead of condemning our imperfection, Scripture provides encouragement for all sorts of circumstances because God knows we will face fearful situations. Instead of being ruled by fear, we are offered another path. We can live in the security and confidence of who God is, what He has done for us, who we are in Him, and what we are promised in Jesus. Our God remains the same, no matter what may come our way.

As you begin this study, take inventory of your own relationship with fear. Then turn to the table of contents to see the reasons why this command is possible to obey. Use the daily questions to reflect on how our very real God is present in every circumstance. My prayer for you, for all of us, is that we would arrive at the end of these three weeks celebrating the freedom found in this simple, repeated command: *Do not fear.*

DESIGN ON PURPOSE

At She Reads Truth, we believe in pairing the inherently beautiful Word of God with the aesthetic beauty it deserves. Each of our resources is thoughtfully and artfully designed to highlight the beauty, goodness, and truth of Scripture in a way that reflects the themes of each curated reading plan.

This Study Book features line art specifically created for this reading plan. Our initial inspiration came from considering the medical graphs generated when someone in distress or fear is under observation. We then created several abstract pieces reflecting on the daily reading to mirror God's character.

The day titles use a prominent Dunbar typeface. Along with the color palette, these additional elements communicate the bold stability and confidence we can have, knowing that God is with us.

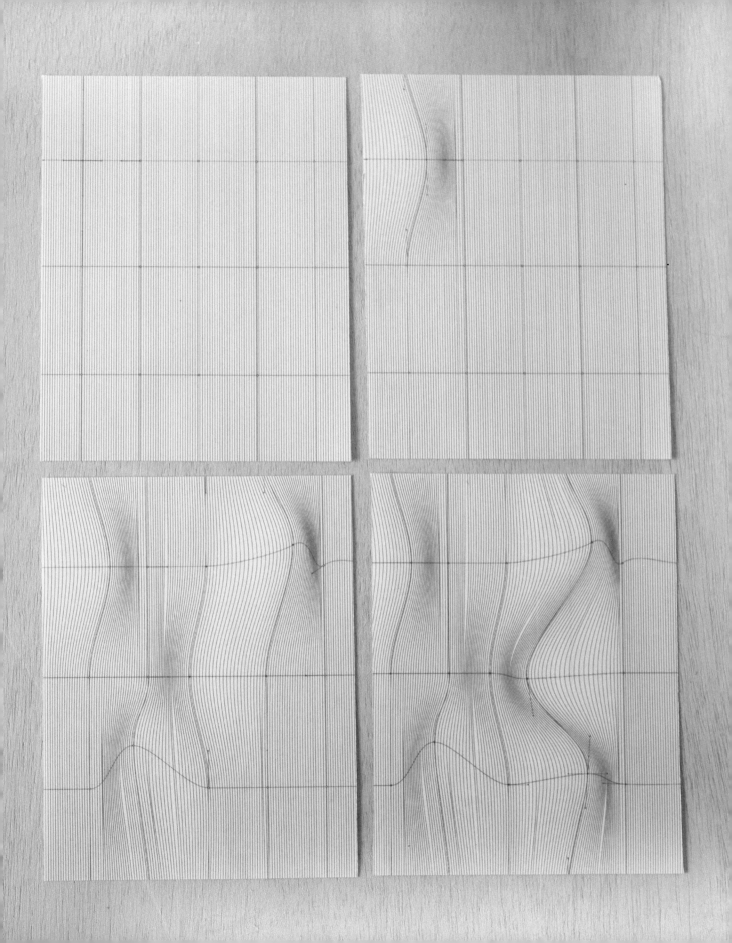

HOW TO USE THIS BOOK

She Reads Truth is a community of women dedicated to
reading the Word of God every day. In this **Do Not Fear**
reading plan, we will look at different narratives from both
the Old and New Testaments, along with complementary
passages from Scripture, to see how God's faithful character
enables believers to respond differently to fear.

READ & REFLECT

Your **Do Not Fear** Study Book
focuses primarily on Scripture,
with bonus resources to
facilitate deeper engagement
with God's Word.

SCRIPTURE READING

Designed for a Monday start, this
Study Book presents daily readings
on fear and God's faithfulness
throughout Scripture.

REFLECTION QUESTIONS

Each weekday features questions
and space for personal reflection.

COMMUNITY & CONVERSATION

You can start reading this book at any time! If you
want to join women from Charleston to Curacao
as they read along with you, the She Reads Truth
community will start Day 1 of **Do Not Fear** on
Monday, February 7, 2022.

 SHE READS TRUTH APP

Devotionals corresponding to each daily reading can
be found in the **Do Not Fear** reading plan on the She
Reads Truth app. New devotionals will be published each
weekday once the plan begins on Monday, February 7,
2022. You can use the app to participate in community
discussion, download free lock screens for Weekly Truth
memorization, and more.

GRACE DAY

Use Saturdays to catch up on your reading, pray, and rest in the presence of the Lord.

WEEKLY TRUTH

Sundays are set aside for Scripture memorization.

See tips for memorizing Scripture on page 108.

EXTRAS

This book features additional tools to help you gain a deeper understanding of the text.

Find a complete list of extras on page 13.

 SHEREADSTRUTH.COM

The **Do Not Fear** reading plan and devotionals will also be available at SheReadsTruth.com as the community reads each day. Invite your family, friends, and neighbors to read along with you!

 SHE READS TRUTH PODCAST

Subscribe to the She Reads Truth podcast and join our founders and their guests each week as they talk about the beauty, goodness, and truth they find in Scripture.

 Podcast episodes 114, 115, and 116 for our **Do Not Fear** *series release on Mondays beginning February 7, 2022.*

KEY

VERSE

Now this is what the Lord says—
the one who created you, Jacob,
and the one who formed you, Israel—
"Do not fear, for I have redeemed you;
I have called you by your name; you are mine.
When you pass through the waters,
I will be with you,
and the rivers will not overwhelm you.
When you walk through the fire,
you will not be scorched,
and the flame will not burn you."

ISAIAH 43:1–2

DO NOT FEAR

Week 1

DAY 1	**For He Will Strengthen You**	14
DAY 2	**For Nothing Is Impossible with God**	21
DAY 3	**For He Is Your Shield**	24
DAY 4	**For He Controls the Wind and the Storm**	28
DAY 5	**For He Is Just**	36
DAY 6	**Grace Day**	40
DAY 7	**Weekly Truth**	42

Week 2

DAY 8	**For He Is Present**	46
DAY 9	**For He Will Fight for You**	50
DAY 10	**For He Sees You and Hears You**	54
DAY 11	**For the Battle Is His**	62
DAY 12	**For He Can Be Trusted**	66
DAY 13	**Grace Day**	72
DAY 14	**Weekly Truth**	74

TABLE OF CONTENTS

Week 3

DAY 15	**For He Will Not Leave You**	78
DAY 16	**For He Rescues and Delivers**	82
DAY 17	**For He Is Your Peace**	86
DAY 18	**For He Sends You**	93
DAY 19	**For He Is Able to Heal**	96
DAY 20	**Grace Day**	100
DAY 21	**Weekly Truth**	102

Extras

Taking Inventory	18
Practicing the Presence of God	32
The Fear of the Lord	58
Hymn: It Is Well with My Soul	70
Prayer: St. Patrick's Breastplate	90
Final Reflection	104
For the Record	112

FOR HE WILL STRENGTHEN YOU

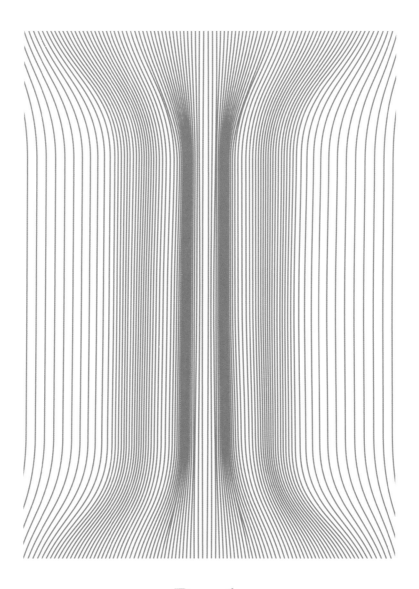

Day 1

THE LORD VERSUS THE NATIONS' GODS

[1] "Be silent before me, coasts and islands!
And let peoples renew their strength.
Let them approach; let them testify;
let's come together for the trial.
[2] Who has stirred up someone from the east?
In righteousness he calls him to serve.
The Lord hands nations over to him,
and he subdues kings.
He makes them like dust with his sword,
like wind-driven stubble with his bow.
[3] He pursues them, going on safely,
hardly touching the path with his feet.
[4] Who has performed and done this,
calling the generations from the beginning?
I am the Lord, the first
and with the last—I am he."

[5] The coasts and islands see and are afraid,
the whole earth trembles.
They approach and arrive.
[6] Each one helps the other,
and says to another, "Take courage!"
[7] The craftsman encourages the metalworker;
the one who flattens with the hammer
encourages the one who strikes the anvil,
saying of the soldering, "It is good."
He fastens it with nails so that it will not fall over.

[8] But you, Israel, my servant,
Jacob, whom I have chosen,
descendant of Abraham, my friend—
[9] I brought you from the ends of the earth
and called you from its farthest corners.
I said to you: You are my servant;
I have chosen you; I haven't rejected you.
[10] Do not fear, for I am with you;
do not be afraid, for I am your God.
I will strengthen you; I will help you;
I will hold on to you with my righteous right hand.

¹¹ Be sure that all who are enraged against you
will be ashamed and disgraced;
those who contend with you
will become as nothing and will perish.
¹² You will look for those who contend with you,
but you will not find them.
Those who war against you
will become absolutely nothing.
¹³ For I am the LORD your God,
who holds your right hand,
who says to you, "Do not fear,
I will help you.
¹⁴ Do not fear, you worm Jacob,
you men of Israel.
I will help you"—
     this is the LORD's declaration.
Your Redeemer is the Holy One of Israel.
¹⁵ See, I will make you into a sharp threshing board,
new, with many teeth.
You will thresh mountains and pulverize them
and make hills into chaff.
¹⁶ You will winnow them
and a wind will carry them away,
a whirlwind will scatter them.
But you will rejoice in the LORD;
you will boast in the Holy One of Israel.

¹⁷ The poor and the needy seek water, but there is none;
their tongues are parched with thirst.
I will answer them.
I am the LORD, the God of Israel. I will not abandon them.
¹⁸ I will open rivers on the barren heights,
and springs in the middle of the plains.
I will turn the desert into a pool
and dry land into springs.
¹⁹ I will plant cedar, acacia, myrtle, and olive trees
in the wilderness.
I will put juniper, elm, and cypress trees together
in the desert,
²⁰ so that all may see and know,
consider and understand,
that the hand of the LORD has done this,
the Holy One of Israel has created it.

ROMANS 8:12–17, 31–39

THE HOLY SPIRIT'S MINISTRIES

¹² So then, brothers and sisters, we are not obligated to the flesh to live according to the flesh, ¹³ because if you live according to the flesh, you are going to die. But if by the Spirit you put to death the deeds of the body, you will live. ¹⁴ For all those led by God's Spirit are God's sons. ¹⁵ For you did not receive a spirit of slavery to fall back into fear. Instead, you received the Spirit of adoption, by whom we cry out, "*Abba*, Father!" ¹⁶ The Spirit himself testifies together with our spirit that we are God's children, ¹⁷ and if children, also heirs—heirs of God and coheirs with Christ—if indeed we suffer with him so that we may also be glorified with him.

…

THE BELIEVER'S TRIUMPH

³¹ What, then, are we to say about these things? If God is for us, who is against us? ³² He did not even spare his own Son but gave him up for us all. How will he not also with him grant us everything? ³³ Who can bring an accusation against God's elect? God is the one who justifies. ³⁴ Who is the one who condemns? Christ Jesus is the one who died, but even more, has been raised; he also is at the right hand of God and intercedes for us. ³⁵ Who can separate us from the love of Christ? Can affliction or distress or persecution or famine or nakedness or danger or sword? ³⁶ As it is written:

> Because of you
> we are being put to death all day long;
> we are counted as sheep to be slaughtered.

³⁷ No, in all these things we are more than conquerors through him who loved us. ³⁸ For I am persuaded that neither death nor life, nor angels nor rulers, nor things present nor things to come, nor powers, ³⁹ nor height nor depth, nor any other created thing will be able to separate us from the love of God that is in Christ Jesus our Lord.

2 TIMOTHY 1:7

For God has not given us a spirit of fear, but one of power, love, and sound judgment.

1 JOHN 4:13–19

[13] This is how we know that we remain in him and he in us: He has given us of his Spirit. [14] And we have seen and we testify that the Father has sent his Son as the world's Savior. [15] Whoever confesses that Jesus is the Son of God—God remains in him and he in God. [16] And we have come to know and to believe the love that God has for us.

God is love, and the one who remains in love remains in God, and God remains in him. [17] In this, love is made complete with us so that we may have confidence in the day of judgment, because as he is, so also are we in this world.

[18] **There is no fear in love; instead, perfect love drives out fear, because fear involves punishment. So the one who fears is not complete in love.**

[19] We love because he first loved us.

TAKING INVENTORY

Use the space below to record situations, circumstances, or anything else that causes you to feel fear.

What is it about each of these things that causes you to be afraid?

Reflect on your emotions, physical response, and actions when you experience fear.
How do you react in moments when you are afraid?

What have you tried in the past to cope with your fears? What has been helpful? What has not?

Write a prayer of expectation for this reading plan.

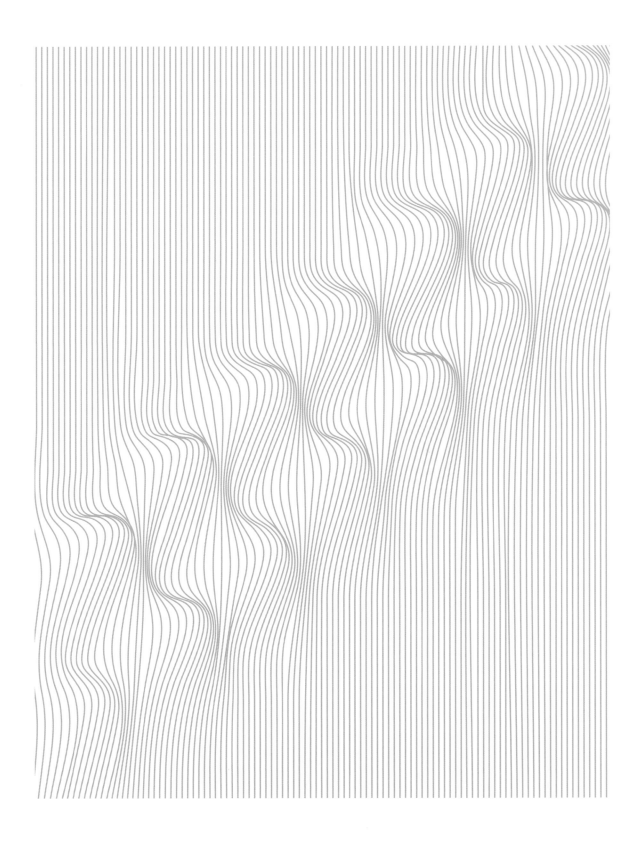

DO NOT FEAR

FOR NOTHING IS IMPOSSIBLE WITH GOD

Day 2

LUKE 1:26–38, 46–55

GABRIEL PREDICTS JESUS'S BIRTH

²⁶ In the sixth month, the angel Gabriel was sent by God to a town in Galilee called Nazareth, ²⁷ to a virgin engaged to a man named Joseph, of the house of David. The virgin's name was Mary. ²⁸ And the angel came to her and said, "Greetings, favored woman! The Lord is with you." ²⁹ But she was deeply troubled by this statement, wondering what kind of greeting this could be. ³⁰ Then the angel told her, "Do not be afraid, Mary, for you have found favor with God. ³¹ Now listen: You will conceive and give birth to a son, and you will name him Jesus. ³² He will be great and will be called the Son of the Most High, and the Lord God will give him the throne of his father David. ³³ He will reign over the house of Jacob forever, and his kingdom will have no end."

³⁴ Mary asked the angel, "How can this be, since I have not had sexual relations with a man?"

³⁵ The angel replied to her, "The Holy Spirit will come upon you, and the power of the Most High will overshadow you. Therefore, the holy one to be born will be called the Son of God. ³⁶ And consider your relative Elizabeth—even she has conceived a son in her old age, and this is the sixth month for her who was called childless. ³⁷ For nothing will be impossible with God."

³⁸ "See, I am the Lord's servant," said Mary. "May it happen to me as you have said." Then the angel left her.

…

MARY'S PRAISE

⁴⁶ And Mary said:

My soul magnifies the Lord,
⁴⁷ and my spirit rejoices in God my Savior,
⁴⁸ because he has looked with favor
on the humble condition of his servant.
Surely, from now on all generations
will call me blessed,
⁴⁹ because the Mighty One
has done great things for me,
and his name is holy.
⁵⁰ His mercy is from generation to generation
on those who fear him.
⁵¹ He has done a mighty deed with his arm;
he has scattered the proud
because of the thoughts of their hearts;
⁵² he has toppled the mighty from their thrones
and exalted the lowly.

⁵³ He has satisfied the hungry with good things
and sent the rich away empty.
⁵⁴ He has helped his servant Israel,
remembering his mercy
⁵⁵ to Abraham and his descendants forever,
just as he spoke to our ancestors.

JOB 42:1–4

¹ Then Job replied to the LORD:

² I know that you can do anything
and no plan of yours can be thwarted.
³ You asked, "Who is this who conceals my counsel
   with ignorance?"
Surely I spoke about things I did not understand,
things too wondrous for me to know.
⁴ You said, "Listen now, and I will speak.
When I question you, you will inform me."

PROVERBS 3:1–7

TRUST THE LORD

¹ My son, don't forget my teaching,
but let your heart keep my commands;
² for they will bring you
many days, a full life, and well-being.
³ Never let loyalty and faithfulness leave you.
Tie them around your neck;
write them on the tablet of your heart.
⁴ Then you will find favor and high regard
with God and people.

⁵ **Trust in the LORD with
all your heart,
and do not rely on your own
understanding;**

⁶ in all your ways know him,
and he will make your paths straight.
⁷ Don't be wise in your own eyes;
fear the LORD and turn away from evil.

EPHESIANS 3:20–21

²⁰ Now to him who is able to do above and beyond all that
we ask or think according to the power that works in us—
²¹ to him be glory in the church and in Christ Jesus to all
generations, forever and ever. Amen.

DAILY RESPONSE

What circumstances in Luke 1 might have led to fear?

What does this passage teach about God's character?

How do today's scriptures speak to similar circumstances
in your own life?

FOR HE IS YOUR SHIELD

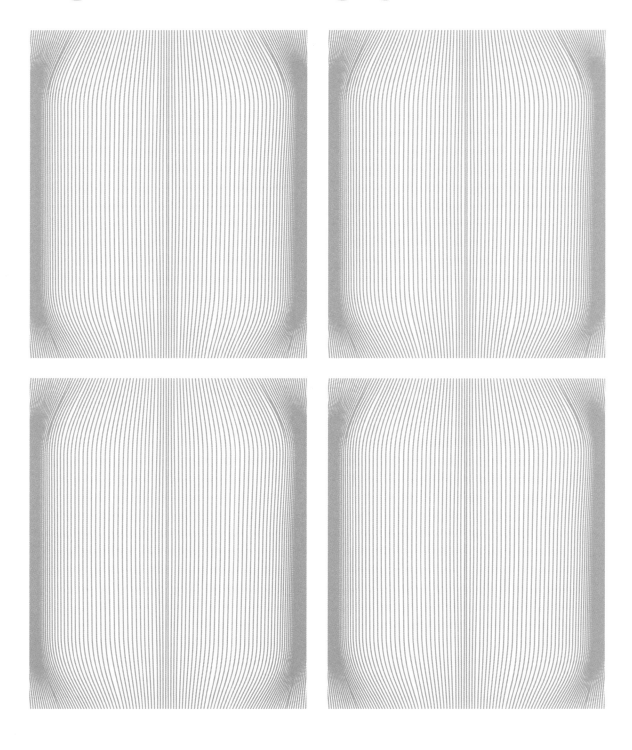

Day 3

GENESIS 15

THE ABRAHAMIC COVENANT

[1] After these events, the word of the LORD came to Abram in a vision:

Do not be afraid, Abram.
I am your shield;

your reward will be very great.

[2] But Abram said, "Lord GOD, what can you give me, since I am childless and the heir of my house is Eliezer of Damascus?" [3] Abram continued, "Look, you have given me no offspring, so a slave born in my house will be my heir."

[4] Now the word of the LORD came to him: "This one will not be your heir; instead, one who comes from your own body will be your heir." [5] He took him outside and said, "Look at the sky and count the stars, if you are able to count them." Then he said to him, "Your offspring will be that numerous."

[6] Abram believed the LORD, and he credited it to him as righteousness.

[7] He also said to him, "I am the LORD who brought you from Ur of the Chaldeans to give you this land to possess."

[8] But he said, "Lord GOD, how can I know that I will possess it?"

[9] He said to him, "Bring me a three-year-old cow, a three-year-old female goat, a three-year-old ram, a turtledove, and a young pigeon."

[10] So he brought all these to him, cut them in half, and laid the pieces opposite each other, but he did not cut the birds in half. [11] Birds of prey came down on the carcasses, but Abram drove them away. [12] As the sun was setting, a deep sleep came over Abram, and suddenly great terror and darkness descended on him.

[13] Then the LORD said to Abram, "Know this for certain: Your offspring will be resident aliens for four hundred years in a land that does not belong to them and will be enslaved and oppressed. [14] However, I will judge the nation they serve, and afterward they will go out with many possessions. [15] But you will go to your ancestors in peace and be buried at a good old age. [16] In the fourth generation they will return here, for the iniquity of the Amorites has not yet reached its full measure."

[17] When the sun had set and it was dark, a smoking fire pot and a flaming torch appeared and passed between the divided animals. [18] On that day the LORD made a covenant with Abram, saying, "I give this land to your offspring, from the Brook of Egypt to the great river, the Euphrates River: [19] the land of the Kenites, Kenizzites, Kadmonites, [20] Hethites, Perizzites, Rephaim, [21] Amorites, Canaanites, Girgashites, and Jebusites."

PSALM 28:6–9

[6] Blessed be the LORD,
for he has heard the sound of my pleading.

[7] The LORD is my strength and
my shield;
my heart trusts in him, and I
am helped.

Therefore my heart celebrates,
and I give thanks to him with my song.

[8] The Lᴏʀᴅ is the strength of his people;
he is a stronghold of salvation for his anointed.
[9] Save your people, bless your possession,
shepherd them, and carry them forever.

ISAIAH 54:1–5

FUTURE GLORY FOR ISRAEL

[1] "Rejoice, childless one, who did not give birth;
burst into song and shout,
you who have not been in labor!
For the children of the desolate one will be more
than the children of the married woman,"
says the Lᴏʀᴅ.
[2] "Enlarge the site of your tent,
and let your tent curtains be stretched out;
do not hold back;
lengthen your ropes,
and drive your pegs deep.
[3] For you will spread out to the right and to the left,
and your descendants will dispossess nations
and inhabit the desolate cities.

[4] "Do not be afraid, for you will not be put to shame;
don't be humiliated, for you will not be disgraced.
For you will forget the shame of your youth,
and you will no longer remember
the disgrace of your widowhood.
[5] Indeed, your husband is your Maker—
his name is the Lᴏʀᴅ of Armies—
and the Holy One of Israel is your Redeemer;
he is called the God of the whole earth."

2 CORINTHIANS 12:9–10

[9] But he said to me, "My grace is sufficient for you, for my
power is perfected in weakness."

Therefore, I will most gladly boast all the more about my
weaknesses, so that Christ's power may reside in me. [10] So I
take pleasure in weaknesses, insults, hardships, persecutions,
and in difficulties, for the sake of Christ. For when I am
weak, then I am strong.

DAILY RESPONSE

What circumstances in Genesis 15 might have led to fear?

What does this passage teach about God's character?

How do today's scriptures speak to similar circumstances
in your own life?

FOR HE CONTROLS THE WIND AND THE STORM

Day 4

MARK 4:35–41

WIND AND WAVES OBEY JESUS

[35] On that day, when evening had come, he told them, "Let's cross over to the other side of the sea." [36] So they left the crowd and took him along since he was in the boat. And other boats were with him. [37] A great windstorm arose, and the waves were breaking over the boat, so that the boat was already being swamped. [38] He was in the stern, sleeping on the cushion. So they woke him up and said to him, "Teacher! Don't you care that we're going to die?"

[39] He got up, rebuked the wind, and said to the sea, "Silence! Be still!" The wind ceased, and there was a great calm. [40] Then he said to them, "Why are you afraid? Do you still have no faith?"

[41] And they were terrified and asked one another, "Who then is this? Even the wind and the sea obey him!"

MATTHEW 14:22–33

WALKING ON THE WATER

22 Immediately he made the disciples get into the boat and go ahead of him to the other side, while he dismissed the crowds. 23 After dismissing the crowds, he went up on the mountain by himself to pray. Well into the night, he was there alone. 24 Meanwhile, the boat was already some distance from land, battered by the waves, because the wind was against them. 25 Jesus came toward them walking on the sea very early in the morning. 26 When the disciples saw him walking on the sea, they were terrified. "It's a ghost!" they said, and they cried out in fear.

27 Immediately Jesus spoke to them. "Have courage! It is I. Don't be afraid."

28 "Lord, if it's you," Peter answered him, "command me to come to you on the water."

29 He said, "Come."

And climbing out of the boat, Peter started walking on the water and came toward Jesus. 30 But when he saw the strength of the wind, he was afraid, and beginning to sink he cried out, "Lord, save me!"

31 Immediately Jesus reached out his hand, caught hold of him, and said to him, "You of little faith, why did you doubt?"

32 When they got into the boat, the wind ceased.

33 **Then those in the boat worshiped him and said, "Truly you are the Son of God."**

PSALM 107:23–32

23 Others went to sea in ships,
conducting trade on the vast water.
24 They saw the LORD's works,
his wondrous works in the deep.
25 He spoke and raised a stormy wind
that stirred up the waves of the sea.
26 Rising up to the sky, sinking down to the depths,
their courage melting away in anguish,
27 they reeled and staggered like a drunkard,
and all their skill was useless.
28 Then they cried out to the LORD in their trouble,
and he brought them out of their distress.
29 He stilled the storm to a whisper,
and the waves of the sea were hushed.
30 They rejoiced when the waves grew quiet.
Then he guided them to the harbor they longed for.
31 Let them give thanks to the LORD
for his faithful love
and his wondrous works for all humanity.
32 Let them exalt him in the assembly of the people
and praise him in the council of the elders.

PSALM 135:5–7

5 For I know that the LORD is great;
our LORD is greater than all gods.
6 The LORD does whatever he pleases
in heaven and on earth,
in the seas and all the depths.
7 He causes the clouds to rise from the ends of the earth.
He makes lightning for the rain
and brings the wind from his storehouses.

ISAIAH 43:1–3

RESTORATION OF ISRAEL

1 Now this is what the LORD says—
the one who created you, Jacob,
and the one who formed you, Israel—
"Do not fear, for I have redeemed you;
I have called you by your name; you are mine.
2 When you pass through the waters,
I will be with you,
and the rivers will not overwhelm you.
When you walk through the fire,

you will not be scorched,
and the flame will not burn you.
³ For I am the LORD your God,
the Holy One of Israel, and your Savior.
I have given Egypt as a ransom for you,
Cush and Seba in your place."

NAHUM 1:3–5

³ The LORD is slow to anger but great in power;
the LORD will never leave the guilty unpunished.
His path is in the whirlwind and storm,
and clouds are the dust beneath his feet.
⁴ He rebukes the sea and dries it up,
and he makes all the rivers run dry.
Bashan and Carmel wither;
even the flower of Lebanon withers.
⁵ The mountains quake before him,
and the hills melt;
the earth trembles at his presence—
the world and all who live in it.

DAILY RESPONSE

What circumstances in Mark 4 and Matthew 14 might have led to fear?

What do these passages teach about God's character?

How do today's scriptures speak to similar circumstances in your own life?

PRACTICING THE PRESENCE OF GOD

Fear is not something we overcome with willpower or our own effort, but instead, something we can face and endure because of God's promises and presence. God's promise to never leave us is our foundation for knowing how to respond when fear creeps in. The Holy Spirit is present in all believers, and Jesus told us He will be with us always (Mt 28:20; Jn 14:16–17). Consider using the tips and reminders on the following pages to help you practice the presence of God.

MAKE INTENTIONAL TIME AND SPACE

Though we often experience the presence of God with other believers at church or other corporate gatherings, we also need to spend time alone with Him.

Choose a time in advance and set an appointment on your calendar. Consider how you can devote parts of your current daily rhythm to trying something new. Carve out fifteen minutes in the morning or before you go to bed, or find a quiet spot during your lunch break.

Decide on a place—in your home, your car, or outdoors.

Minimize distractions. Turn off your television, phone, and other devices. If you can, close your eyes to help you focus.

MEDITATE ON GOD'S WORD

Meditating on God's Word means taking time to slowly read and think about Scripture and what it tells us about who God is. As you read through these passages about responding to fear, pause to slowly take them in or reread those that stand out to you.

Many Christians find praying the words of Scripture to be a powerful experience, especially in times of fear or grief.

Memorizing individual verses and longer passages helps us internalize what we have read. When we memorize Scripture, we carry God's Word with us and are better prepared for the trials we are sure to face. Consider memorizing the Weekly Truth passage on page 43 as a reminder of God's faithfulness.

Name God's character traits that you noted in your Scripture reading and spend time reflecting on them.

PRAY

Ask God to meet with you, speak to you, and show you your circumstances in a fresh way. God is with us always, so we can talk with Him all the time. When we talk to God, we can be confident that He hears and answers us (Jr 29:12–13; 1Jn 5:14).

Thank God for who He is and how He has provided for you (Ps 103:1–2). Thank God for the promises He has made to His people.

Pray for the needs of the greater Church and the world (Mt 6:9–13). Pray for your own personal needs (Mk 10:51). Pray for the fears you are currently facing.

As the apostle Paul said, we are to "pray constantly" (1Th 5:17). Think of ways you can remind yourself to pause and pray throughout the day, like setting an alert on your phone or placing a verse where you'll see it often.

Choose a prayer, blessing, or poem about God that someone else has written as a guide.

Spend time not only talking to God, but listening as well. Jesus said that His sheep know His voice (Jn 10:4). Remember, if listening to God in this way is new for you, it may be hard to be silent at first. Don't be discouraged. It will get easier with time.

WORSHIP

Being in God's presence doesn't always look like sitting still and being quiet. There are many different ways to embrace God's presence through worship.

Walk, dance, sing, or play a musical instrument (2Sm 6:14; Ps 149:3).

Engage in corporate worship with your local church (Ac 2:42–45).

Participate in the Lord's Supper (1Co 11:23–26).

Serve the needs of those around you (Mt 25:35–40).

Praise God for His nearness or lament that He doesn't feel as near as you would like (Ps 34; 10).

FOR HE
IS JUST

Day 5

NUMBERS 13:17–33

17 When Moses sent them to scout out the land of Canaan, he told them, "Go up this way to the Negev, then go up into the hill country. 18 See what the land is like, and whether the people who live there are strong or weak, few or many. 19 Is the land they live in good or bad? Are the cities they live in encampments or fortifications? 20 Is the land fertile or unproductive? Are there trees in it or not? Be courageous. Bring back some fruit from the land." It was the season for the first ripe grapes.

21 So they went up and scouted out the land from the Wilderness of Zin as far as Rehob near the entrance to Hamath. 22 They went up through the Negev and came to Hebron, where Ahiman, Sheshai, and Talmai, the descendants of Anak, were living. Hebron was built seven years before Zoan in Egypt. 23 When they came to Eshcol Valley, they cut down a branch with a single cluster of grapes, which was carried on a pole by two men. They also took some pomegranates and figs. 24 That place was called Eshcol Valley because of the cluster of grapes the Israelites cut there. 25 At the end of forty days they returned from scouting out the land.

REPORT ABOUT CANAAN

26 The men went back to Moses, Aaron, and the entire Israelite community in the Wilderness of Paran at Kadesh. They brought back a report for them and the whole community, and they showed them the fruit of the land. 27 They reported to Moses, "We went into the land where you sent us. Indeed it is flowing with milk and honey, and here is some of its fruit. 28 However, the people living in the land are strong, and the cities are large and fortified. We also saw the descendants of Anak there. 29 The Amalekites are living in the land of the Negev; the Hethites, Jebusites, and Amorites live in the hill country; and the Canaanites live by the sea and along the Jordan."

30 Then Caleb quieted the people in the presence of Moses and said, "Let's go up now and take possession of the land because we can certainly conquer it!"

31 But the men who had gone up with him responded, "We can't attack the people because they are stronger than we are!" 32 So they gave a negative report to the Israelites about the land they had scouted: "The land we passed through to explore is one that devours its inhabitants, and all the people we saw in it are men of great size. 33 We even saw the Nephilim there—the descendants of Anak come from the Nephilim! To ourselves we seemed like grasshoppers, and we must have seemed the same to them."

NUMBERS 14:1–24

ISRAEL'S REFUSAL TO ENTER CANAAN

1 Then the whole community broke into loud cries, and the people wept that night. 2 All the Israelites complained about Moses and Aaron, and the whole community told them, "If only we had died in the land of Egypt, or if only we had died in this wilderness! 3 Why is the LORD bringing us into this land to die by the sword? Our wives and children will become plunder. Wouldn't it be better for us to go back to Egypt?" 4 So they said to one another, "Let's appoint a leader and go back to Egypt."

5 Then Moses and Aaron fell facedown in front of the whole assembly of the Israelite community. 6 Joshua son of Nun and Caleb son of Jephunneh, who were among those who scouted out the land, tore their clothes 7 and said to the entire Israelite community, "The land we passed through and explored is an extremely good land. 8 If the LORD is pleased with us, he will bring us into this land, a land flowing with milk and honey, and give it to us. 9 Only don't rebel against the LORD, and don't be afraid of the people of the land, for we will devour them. Their protection has been removed from them, and the LORD is with us. Don't be afraid of them!"

10 While the whole community threatened to stone them, the glory of the LORD appeared to all the Israelites at the tent of meeting.

GOD'S JUDGMENT OF ISRAEL'S REBELLION

11 The LORD said to Moses, "How long will these people despise me? How long will they not trust in me despite all the signs I have performed among them? 12 I will strike them with a plague and destroy them. Then I will make you into a greater and mightier nation than they are."

¹³ But Moses replied to the LORD, "The Egyptians will hear about it, for by your strength you brought up this people from them. ¹⁴ They will tell it to the inhabitants of this land. They have heard that you, LORD, are among these people, how you, LORD, are seen face to face, how your cloud stands over them, and how you go before them in a pillar of cloud by day and in a pillar of fire by night. ¹⁵ If you kill this people with a single blow, the nations that have heard of your fame will declare, ¹⁶ 'Since the LORD wasn't able to bring this people into the land he swore to give them, he has slaughtered them in the wilderness.'

¹⁷ "So now, may my Lord's power be magnified just as you have spoken:

¹⁸ The LORD is slow to anger and abounding in faithful love, forgiving iniquity and rebellion. But he will not leave the guilty unpunished, bringing the consequences of the fathers' iniquity on the children to the third and fourth generation.

¹⁹ Please pardon the iniquity of this people, in keeping with the greatness of your faithful love, just as you have forgiven them from Egypt until now."

²⁰ The LORD responded, "I have pardoned them as you requested. ²¹ Yet as I live and as the whole earth is filled with the LORD's glory, ²² none of the men who have seen my glory and the signs I performed in Egypt and in the wilderness, and have tested me these ten times and did not obey me, ²³ will ever see the land I swore to give their ancestors. None of those who have despised me will see it. ²⁴ But since my servant Caleb has a different spirit and has remained loyal to me, I will bring him into the land where he has gone, and his descendants will inherit it.

JEREMIAH 32:17–19

¹⁷ Oh, Lord GOD! You yourself made the heavens and earth by your great power and with your outstretched arm. Nothing is too difficult for you! ¹⁸ You show faithful love to thousands but lay the fathers' iniquity on their sons' laps after them, great and mighty God whose name is the LORD of Armies, ¹⁹ the one great in counsel and powerful in action. Your eyes are on all the ways of the children of men in order to reward each person according to his ways and as the result of his actions.

PHILIPPIANS 4:6–7

⁶ Don't worry about anything, but in everything, through prayer and petition with thanksgiving, present your requests to God. ⁷ And the peace of God, which surpasses all understanding, will guard your hearts and minds in Christ Jesus.

DAILY RESPONSE

What circumstances in Numbers 13 and 14 might have
led to fear?

What do these passages teach about God's character?

How do today's scriptures speak to similar circumstances
in your own life?

GRACE

DAY

Take this day to catch up on your reading, pray, and rest in the presence of the Lord.

6

For God has not given us a spirit of fear, but one of power, love, and sound judgment.

2 TIMOTHY 1:7

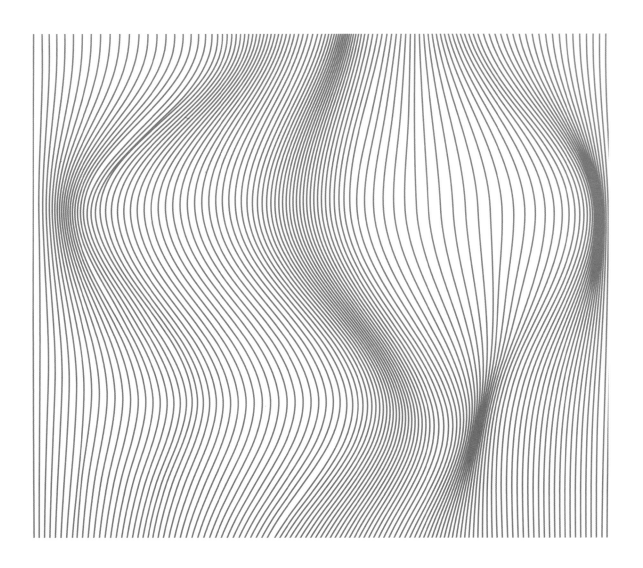

WEEKLY TRUTH

Day 7

Scripture is God-breathed and true. When we memorize it, we carry the good news of Jesus with us wherever we go.

During this study, we will memorize the key passage for this plan, Isaiah 43:1–2. Here we find reassurance that we don't have to be afraid, because the God who redeemed us and calls us His own is with us. This week we will memorize verse 1.

Now this is what the LORD says—the one who created you, Jacob, and the one who formed you, Israel—"Do not fear, for I have redeemed you; I have called you by your name; you are mine. When you pass through the waters, I will be with you, and the rivers will not overwhelm you. When you walk through the fire, you will not be scorched, and the flame will not burn you."

ISAIAH 43:1–2

See tips for memorizing Scripture on page 108!

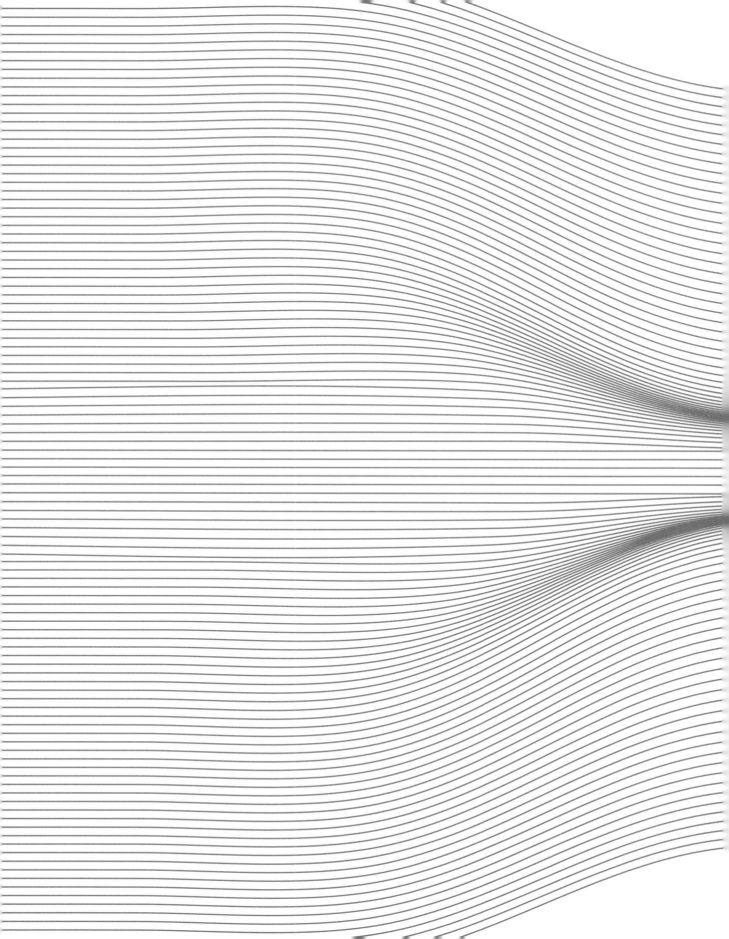

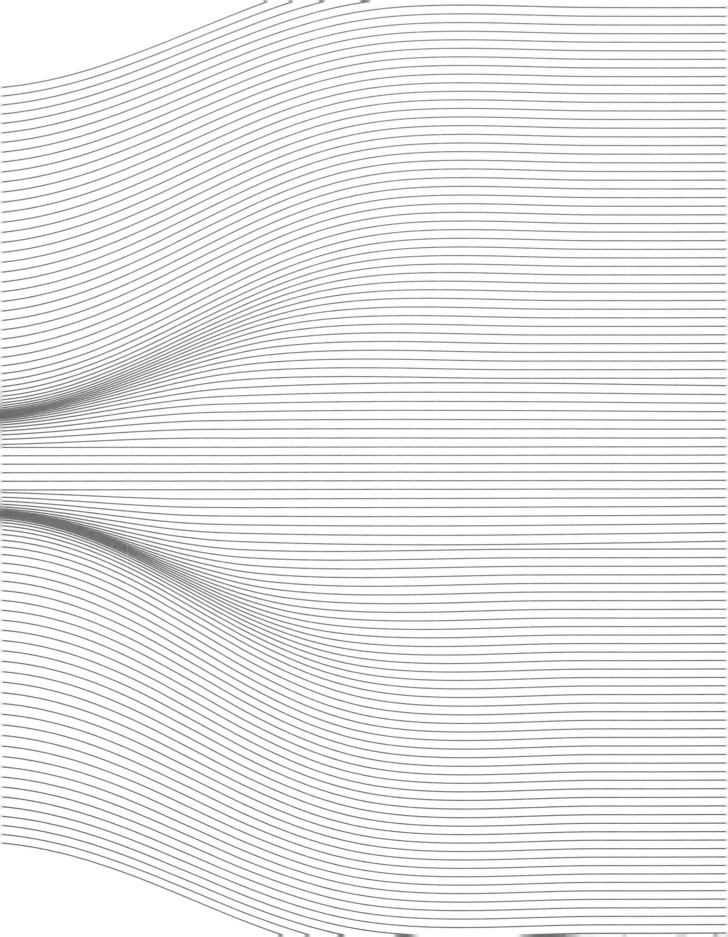

FOR HE IS PRESENT

Day 8

1 KINGS 18:17–46

[17] When Ahab saw Elijah, Ahab said to him, "Is that you, the one ruining Israel?"

[18] He replied, "I have not ruined Israel, but you and your father's family have, because you have abandoned the LORD's commands and followed the Baals. [19] Now summon all Israel to meet me at Mount Carmel, along with the 450 prophets of Baal and the 400 prophets of Asherah who eat at Jezebel's table."

ELIJAH AT MOUNT CARMEL

[20] So Ahab summoned all the Israelites and gathered the prophets at Mount Carmel. [21] Then Elijah approached all the people and said, "How long will you waver between two opinions? If the LORD is God, follow him. But if Baal, follow him." But the people didn't answer him a word.

[22] Then Elijah said to the people, "I am the only remaining prophet of the LORD, but Baal's prophets are 450 men. [23] Let two bulls be given to us. They are to choose one bull for themselves, cut it in pieces, and place it on the wood but not light the fire. I will prepare the other bull and place it on the wood but not light the fire. [24] Then you call on the name of your god, and I will call on the name of the LORD. The God who answers with fire, he is God."

All the people answered, "That's fine."

[25] Then Elijah said to the prophets of Baal, "Since you are so numerous, choose for yourselves one bull and prepare it first. Then call on the name of your god but don't light the fire."

[26] So they took the bull that he gave them, prepared it, and called on the name of Baal from morning until noon, saying, "Baal, answer us!" But there was no sound; no one answered. Then they danced around the altar they had made.

[27] At noon Elijah mocked them. He said, "Shout loudly, for he's a god! Maybe he's thinking it over; maybe he has wandered away; or maybe he's on the road. Perhaps he's

sleeping and will wake up!" ²⁸ They shouted loudly, and cut themselves with knives and spears, according to their custom, until blood gushed over them. ²⁹ All afternoon they kept on raving until the offering of the evening sacrifice, but there was no sound; no one answered, no one paid attention.

³⁰ Then Elijah said to all the people, "Come near me." So all the people approached him. Then he repaired the LORD's altar that had been torn down: ³¹ Elijah took twelve stones—according to the number of the tribes of the sons of Jacob, to whom the word of the LORD had come, saying, "Israel will be your name"— ³² and he built an altar with the stones in the name of the LORD. Then he made a trench around the altar large enough to hold about four gallons. ³³ Next, he arranged the wood, cut up the bull, and placed it on the wood. He said, "Fill four water pots with water and pour it on the offering to be burned and on the wood." ³⁴ Then he said, "A second time!" and they did it a second time. And then he said, "A third time!" and they did it a third time. ³⁵ So the water ran all around the altar; he even filled the trench with water.

³⁶ At the time for offering the evening sacrifice, the prophet Elijah approached the altar and said, "LORD, the God of Abraham, Isaac, and Israel, today let it be known that you are God in Israel and I am your servant, and that at your word I have done all these things. ³⁷ Answer me, LORD! Answer me so that this people will know that you, the LORD, are God and that you have turned their hearts back."

³⁸ Then the LORD's fire fell and consumed the burnt offering, the wood, the stones, and the dust, and it licked up the water that was in the trench. ³⁹ When all the people saw it, they fell facedown and said, "The LORD, he is God! The LORD, he is God!"

⁴⁰ Then Elijah ordered them, "Seize the prophets of Baal! Do not let even one of them escape." So they seized them, and Elijah brought them down to the Wadi Kishon and slaughtered them there. ⁴¹ Elijah said to Ahab, "Go up, eat and drink, for there is the sound of a rainstorm."

⁴² So Ahab went to eat and drink, but Elijah went up to the summit of Carmel. He bent down on the ground and put his face between his knees. ⁴³ Then he said to his servant, "Go up and look toward the sea."

So he went up, looked, and said, "There's nothing."

Seven times Elijah said, "Go back."

⁴⁴ On the seventh time, he reported, "There's a cloud as small as a man's hand coming up from the sea."

Then Elijah said, "Go and tell Ahab, 'Get your chariot ready and go down so the rain doesn't stop you.'"

⁴⁵ In a little while, the sky grew dark with clouds and wind, and there was a downpour. So Ahab got in his chariot and went to Jezreel. ⁴⁶ The power of the LORD was on Elijah, and he tucked his mantle under his belt and ran ahead of Ahab to the entrance of Jezreel.

1 KINGS 19:1–16

ELIJAH'S JOURNEY TO HOREB

¹ Ahab told Jezebel everything that Elijah had done and how he had killed all the prophets with the sword. ² So Jezebel sent a messenger to Elijah, saying, "May the gods punish me and do so severely if I don't make your life like the life of one of them by this time tomorrow!"

³ Then Elijah became afraid and immediately ran for his life. When he came to Beer-sheba that belonged to Judah, he left his servant there, ⁴ but he went on a day's journey into the wilderness. He sat down under a broom tree and prayed that he might die. He said, "I have had enough! LORD, take my life, for I'm no better than my ancestors." ⁵ Then he lay down and slept under the broom tree.

Suddenly, an angel touched him. The angel told him, "Get up and eat." ⁶ Then he looked, and there at his head was a loaf of bread baked over hot stones, and a jug of water. So he ate and drank and lay down again. ⁷ Then the angel of the LORD returned for a second time and touched him. He said, "Get up and eat, or the journey will be too much for you." ⁸ So he got up, ate, and drank. Then on the strength from that food, he walked forty days and forty nights to Horeb, the mountain of God. ⁹ He entered a cave there and spent the night.

ELIJAH'S ENCOUNTER WITH THE LORD

Suddenly, the word of the LORD came to him, and he said to him, "What are you doing here, Elijah?"

¹⁰ He replied, "I have been very zealous for the LORD God of Armies, but the Israelites have abandoned your covenant, torn down your altars, and killed your prophets with the sword. I alone am left, and they are looking for me to take my life."

¹¹ Then he said, "Go out and stand on the mountain in the LORD's presence."

At that moment, the LORD passed by. A great and mighty wind was tearing at the mountains and was shattering cliffs before the LORD, but the LORD was not in the wind. After the wind there was an earthquake, but the LORD was not in the earthquake. ¹² After the earthquake there was a fire, but the LORD was not in the fire.

And after the fire there was a voice, a soft whisper.

¹³ When Elijah heard it, he wrapped his face in his mantle and went out and stood at the entrance of the cave.

Suddenly, a voice came to him and said, "What are you doing here, Elijah?"

¹⁴ "I have been very zealous for the LORD God of Armies," he replied, "but the Israelites have abandoned your covenant, torn down your altars, and killed your prophets with the sword. I alone am left, and they're looking for me to take my life."

¹⁵ Then the LORD said to him, "Go and return by the way you came to the Wilderness of Damascus. When you arrive, you are to anoint Hazael as king over Aram. ¹⁶ You are to anoint Jehu son of Nimshi as king over Israel and Elisha son of Shaphat from Abel-meholah as prophet in your place."

PSALM 56:1–4

A CALL FOR GOD'S PROTECTION

For the choir director: according to "A Silent Dove Far Away." A Miktam of David. When the Philistines seized him in Gath.

¹ Be gracious to me, God, for a man is trampling me;
he fights and oppresses me all day long.
² My adversaries trample me all day,
for many arrogantly fight against me.

³ When I am afraid,
I will trust in you.
⁴ In God, whose word I praise,
in God I trust; I will not be afraid.
What can mere mortals do to me?

1 PETER 3:13–17

UNDESERVED SUFFERING

¹³ Who then will harm you if you are devoted to what is good? ¹⁴ But even if you should suffer for righteousness, you are blessed. Do not fear them or be intimidated, ¹⁵ but in your hearts regard Christ the Lord as holy, ready at any time to give a defense to anyone who asks you for a reason for the hope that is in you. ¹⁶ Yet do this with gentleness and reverence, keeping a clear conscience, so that when you are accused, those who disparage your good conduct in Christ will be put to shame. ¹⁷ For it is better to suffer for doing good, if that should be God's will, than for doing evil.

DAILY RESPONSE

What circumstances in 1 Kings 18 and 19 might have led
to fear?

What do these passages teach about God's character?

How do today's scriptures speak to similar circumstances
in your own life?

FOR HE WILL FIGHT FOR YOU

Day 9

NEHEMIAH 2:1–6

NEHEMIAH SENT TO JERUSALEM

[1] During the month of Nisan in the twentieth year of King Artaxerxes, when wine was set before him, I took the wine and gave it to the king. I had never been sad in his presence, [2] so the king said to me, "Why do you look so sad, when you aren't sick? This is nothing but sadness of heart."

I was overwhelmed with fear [3] and replied to the king, "May the king live forever! Why should I not be sad when the city where my ancestors are buried lies in ruins and its gates have been destroyed by fire?"

[4] Then the king asked me, "What is your request?"

So I prayed to the God of the heavens [5] and answered the king, "If it pleases the king, and if your servant has found favor with you, send me to Judah and to the city where my ancestors are buried, so that I may rebuild it."

[6] The king, with the queen seated beside him, asked me, "How long will your journey take, and when will you return?" So I gave him a definite time, and it pleased the king to send me.

NEHEMIAH 4

PROGRESS IN SPITE OF OPPOSITION

[1] When Sanballat heard that we were rebuilding the wall, he became furious. He mocked the Jews [2] before his colleagues and the powerful men of Samaria and said, "What are these pathetic Jews doing? Can they restore it by themselves? Will they offer sacrifices? Will they ever finish it? Can they bring these burnt stones back to life from the mounds of rubble?" [3] Then Tobiah the Ammonite, who was beside him, said, "Indeed, even if a fox climbed up what they are building, he would break down their stone wall!"

[4] Listen, our God, for we are despised. Make their insults return on their own heads and let them be taken as plunder to a land of captivity. [5] Do not cover their guilt or let their sin be erased from your sight, because they have angered the builders.

[6] So we rebuilt the wall until the entire wall was joined together up to half its height, for the people had the will to keep working.

[7] When Sanballat, Tobiah, and the Arabs, Ammonites, and Ashdodites heard that the repair to the walls of Jerusalem was progressing and that the gaps were being closed, they became furious. [8] They all plotted together to come and fight against Jerusalem and throw it into confusion. [9] So we prayed to our God and stationed a guard because of them day and night.

[10] In Judah, it was said:

The strength of the laborer fails,
since there is so much rubble.
We will never be able
to rebuild the wall.

[11] And our enemies said, "They won't realize it until we're among them and can kill them and stop the work." [12] When the Jews who lived nearby arrived, they said to us time and again, "Everywhere you turn, they attack us." [13] So I stationed people behind the lowest sections of the wall, at the vulnerable areas. I stationed them by families with their swords, spears, and bows. [14] After I made an inspection, I stood up and said to the nobles, the officials, and the rest of the people, "Don't be afraid of them. Remember the great and awe-inspiring Lord, and fight for your countrymen, your sons and daughters, your wives and homes."

SWORD AND TROWEL

[15] When our enemies heard that we knew their scheme and that God had frustrated it, every one of us returned to his own work on the wall. [16] From that day on, half of my men did the work while the other half held spears, shields, bows, and armor. The officers supported all the people of Judah, [17] who were rebuilding the wall. The laborers who carried the loads worked with one hand and held a weapon with the other. [18] Each of the builders had his sword strapped around his waist while he was building, and the one who sounded the ram's horn was beside me. [19] Then I said to the nobles, the officials, and the rest of the people, "The work is enormous and spread out, and we are separated far from one another

along the wall. [20] Wherever you hear the sound of the ram's horn, rally to us there. Our God will fight for us!" [21] So we continued the work, while half of the men were holding spears from daybreak until the stars came out. [22] At that time, I also said to the people, "Let everyone and his servant spend the night inside Jerusalem, so that they can stand guard by night and work by day." [23] And I, my brothers, my servants, and the men of the guard with me never took off our clothes. Each carried his weapon, even when washing.

1 CHRONICLES 28:20

Then David said to his son Solomon, "Be strong and courageous, and do the work. Don't be afraid or discouraged, for the Lord God, my God, is with you. He won't leave you or abandon you until all the work for the service of the Lord's house is finished."

PSALM 27

MY STRONGHOLD

Of David.

[1] The Lord is my light and my salvation—
whom should I fear?
The Lord is the stronghold of my life—
whom should I dread?
[2] When evildoers came against me to devour my flesh,
my foes and my enemies stumbled and fell.
[3] Though an army deploys against me,
my heart will not be afraid;
though a war breaks out against me,
I will still be confident.

[4] I have asked one thing from the Lord;
it is what I desire:
to dwell in the house of the Lord
all the days of my life,
gazing on the beauty of the Lord
and seeking him in his temple.
[5] For he will conceal me in his shelter
in the day of adversity;
he will hide me under the cover of his tent;
he will set me high on a rock.

[6] Then my head will be high
above my enemies around me;
I will offer sacrifices in his tent with shouts of joy.
I will sing and make music to the Lord.

[7] Lord, hear my voice when I call;
be gracious to me and answer me.
[8] My heart says this about you:
"Seek his face."
Lord, I will seek your face.
[9] Do not hide your face from me;
do not turn your servant away in anger.
You have been my helper;
do not leave me or abandon me,
God of my salvation.
[10] Even if my father and mother abandon me,
the Lord cares for me.

[11] Because of my adversaries,
show me your way, Lord,
and lead me on a level path.
[12] Do not give me over to the will of my foes,
for false witnesses rise up against me,
breathing violence.

[13] I am certain that I will see the Lord's goodness
in the land of the living.
[14] Wait for the Lord;
be strong, and let your heart be courageous.
Wait for the Lord.

MATTHEW 10:26–30

FEAR GOD

[26] "Therefore, don't be afraid of them, since there is nothing covered that won't be uncovered and nothing hidden that won't be made known. [27] What I tell you in the dark, speak in the light. What you hear in a whisper, proclaim on the housetops. [28] Don't fear those who kill the body but are not able to kill the soul; rather, fear him who is able to destroy both soul and body in hell. [29] Aren't two sparrows sold for a penny? Yet not one of them falls to the ground without your Father's consent. [30] But even the hairs of your head have all been counted."

DAILY RESPONSE

What circumstances in Nehemiah 2 and 4 might have led to fear?

What do these passages teach about God's character?

How do today's scriptures speak to similar circumstances in your own life?

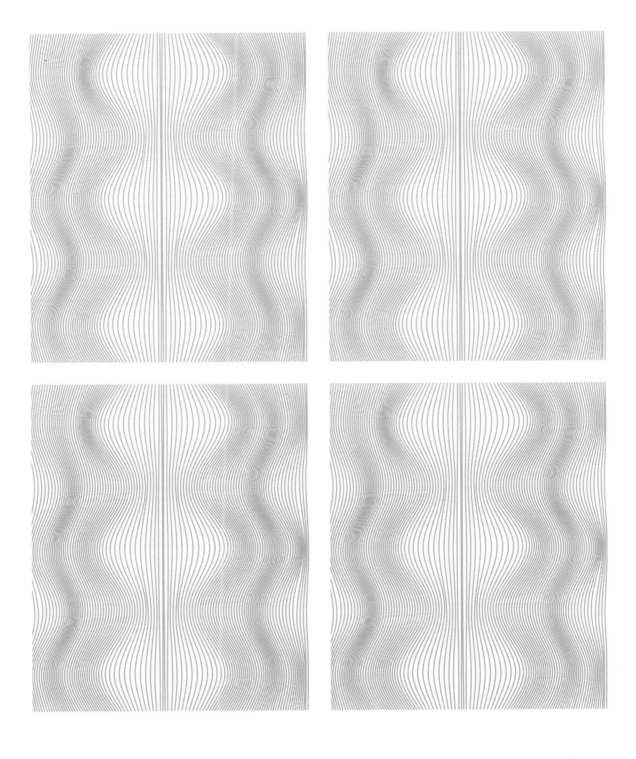

GENESIS 16:1–16

HAGAR AND ISHMAEL

¹ Abram's wife, Sarai, had not borne any children for him, but she owned an Egyptian slave named Hagar. ² Sarai said to Abram, "Since the LORD has prevented me from bearing children, go to my slave; perhaps through her I can build a family." And Abram agreed to what Sarai said. ³ So Abram's wife, Sarai, took Hagar, her Egyptian slave, and gave her to her husband, Abram, as a wife for him. This happened after Abram had lived in the land of Canaan ten years. ⁴ He slept with Hagar, and she became pregnant. When she saw that she was pregnant, her mistress became contemptible to her. ⁵ Then Sarai said to Abram, "You are responsible for my suffering! I put my slave in your arms, and when she saw that she was pregnant, I became contemptible to her. May the LORD judge between me and you."

⁶ Abram replied to Sarai, "Here, your slave is in your power; do whatever you want with her." Then Sarai mistreated her so much that she ran away from her.

⁷ The angel of the LORD found her by a spring in the wilderness, the spring on the way to Shur. ⁸ He said, "Hagar, slave of Sarai, where have you come from and where are you going?"

She replied, "I'm running away from my mistress Sarai."

⁹ The angel of the LORD said to her, "Go back to your mistress and submit to her authority." ¹⁰ The angel of the LORD said to her, "I will greatly multiply your offspring, and they will be too many to count."

¹¹ The angel of the LORD said to her, "You have conceived and will have a son. You will name him Ishmael, for the LORD has heard your cry of affliction. ¹² This man will be like a wild donkey. His hand will be against everyone, and everyone's hand will be against him; he will settle near all his relatives."

¹³ So she named the LORD who spoke to her: "You are El-roi," for she said, "In this place, have I actually seen the one who sees me?" ¹⁴ That is why the well is called Beer-lahai-roi. It is between Kadesh and Bered.

¹⁵ So Hagar gave birth to Abram's son, and Abram named his son (whom Hagar bore) Ishmael. ¹⁶ Abram was eighty-six years old when Hagar bore Ishmael to him.

GENESIS 21:1–3, 8–21

THE BIRTH OF ISAAC

¹ The LORD came to Sarah as he had said, and the LORD did for Sarah what he had promised. ² Sarah became pregnant and bore a son to Abraham in his old age, at the appointed time God had told him. ³ Abraham named his son who was born to him—the one Sarah bore to him—Isaac.

…

HAGAR AND ISHMAEL SENT AWAY

⁸ The child grew and was weaned, and Abraham held a great feast on the day Isaac was weaned. ⁹ But Sarah saw the son mocking—the one Hagar the Egyptian had borne to Abraham. ¹⁰ So she said to Abraham, "Drive out this slave with her son, for the son of this slave will not be a coheir with my son Isaac!"

¹¹ This was very distressing to Abraham because of his son. ¹² But God said to Abraham, "Do not be distressed about the boy and about your slave. Whatever Sarah says to you, listen to her, because your offspring will be traced through Isaac, ¹³ and I will also make a nation of the slave's son because he is your offspring."

¹⁴ Early in the morning Abraham got up, took bread and a waterskin, put them on Hagar's shoulders, and sent her and the boy away. She left and wandered in the Wilderness of Beer-sheba. ¹⁵ When the water in the skin was gone, she left the boy under one of the bushes ¹⁶ and went and sat at a distance, about a bowshot away, for she said, "I can't

bear to watch the boy die!" While she sat at a distance, she wept loudly.

[17] God heard the boy crying, and the angel of God called to Hagar from heaven and said to her, "What's wrong, Hagar? Don't be afraid, for God has heard the boy crying from the place where he is. [18] Get up, help the boy up, and grasp his hand, for I will make him a great nation." [19] Then God opened her eyes, and she saw a well. So she went and filled the waterskin and gave the boy a drink. [20] God was with the boy, and he grew; he settled in the wilderness and became an archer. [21] He settled in the Wilderness of Paran, and his mother got a wife for him from the land of Egypt.

PSALM 34:1–10

THE LORD DELIVERS THE RIGHTEOUS

Concerning David, when he pretended to be insane in the presence of Abimelech, who drove him out, and he departed.

[1] I will bless the LORD at all times;
his praise will always be on my lips.
[2] I will boast in the LORD;
the humble will hear and be glad.
[3] Proclaim the LORD's greatness with me;
let us exalt his name together.

[4] I sought the LORD, and he answered me
and rescued me from all my fears.
[5] Those who look to him are radiant with joy;
their faces will never be ashamed.
[6] This poor man cried, and the LORD heard him
and saved him from all his troubles.
[7] The angel of the LORD encamps
around those who fear him, and rescues them.

[8] Taste and see that the LORD is good.
How happy is the person who takes refuge in him!
[9] You who are his holy ones, fear the LORD,
for those who fear him lack nothing.
[10] Young lions lack food and go hungry,
but those who seek the LORD
will not lack any good thing.

LAMENTATIONS 3:55–60

QOPH

[55] I called on your name, LORD,
from the depths of the pit.
[56] You heard my plea:
Do not ignore my cry for relief.
[57] You came near whenever I called you;
you said, "Do not be afraid."

RESH

[58] You championed my cause, Lord;
you redeemed my life.
[59] LORD, you saw the wrong done to me;
judge my case.
[60] You saw all their vengefulness,
all their plots against me.

MATTHEW 6:25–34

THE CURE FOR ANXIETY

[25] "Therefore I tell you: Don't worry about your life, what you will eat or what you will drink; or about your body, what you will wear. Isn't life more than food and the body more than clothing? [26] Consider the birds of the sky: They don't sow or reap or gather into barns, yet your heavenly Father feeds them. Aren't you worth more than they? [27] Can any of you add one moment to his life span by worrying? [28] And why do you worry about clothes? Observe how the wildflowers of the field grow: They don't labor or spin thread. [29] Yet I tell you that not even Solomon in all his splendor was adorned like one of these. [30] If that's how God clothes the grass of the field, which is here today and thrown into the furnace tomorrow, won't he do much more for you—you of little faith? [31] So don't worry, saying, 'What will we eat?' or 'What will we drink?' or 'What will we wear?' [32] For the Gentiles eagerly seek all these things, and your heavenly Father knows that you need them. [33] But seek first the kingdom of God and his righteousness, and all these things will be provided for you. [34] Therefore don't worry about tomorrow, because tomorrow will worry about itself. Each day has enough trouble of its own."

DAILY RESPONSE

What circumstances in Genesis 16 and 21 might have led
to fear?

What do these passages teach about God's character?

How do today's scriptures speak to similar circumstances
in your own life?

THE FEAR OF THE LORD

The Bible offers instructions for living in the world God created, emphasizing that "the fear of the Lord" is the source of all wisdom and the connection between character and consequences.

Fearing God means approaching Him with an attitude of reverence for His character and a posture of obedience to His Word. Here are some key verses, found primarily in the Bible's books of Wisdom Literature, that give us more detail about what the fear of the Lord means and how it shapes the way we live.

THE FEAR OF THE LORD…	SCRIPTURE	ADDITIONAL READING
IS THE SOURCE AND ESSENCE OF WISDOM	The fear of the Lord is the beginning of wisdom, and the knowledge of the Holy One is understanding. **Proverbs 9:10** He said to mankind, "The fear of the Lord—that is wisdom. And to turn from evil is understanding." **Job 28:28**	Ps 111:10; Pr 1:7, 29; 2:5; 15:33
DESCRIBES THE CHARACTER OF JESUS	The Spirit of the Lord will rest on him—a Spirit of wisdom and understanding, a Spirit of counsel and strength, a Spirit of knowledge and of the fear of the Lord. His delight will be in the fear of the Lord… **Isaiah 11:2–3**	1Co 1:30; Col 2:2–3
PROVOKES TERROR AT GOD'S PRESENCE	The fear of the Lord fell on all the kingdoms of the lands surrounding Judah, so that they did not go to war against Jehoshaphat. **2 Chronicles 17:10 NIV**	2Ch 14:14; 19:7

IS CONNECTED WITH KNOWING GOD'S WORD	The fear of the LORD is pure, enduring forever; the ordinances of the LORD are reliable and altogether righteous. **Psalm 19:9**	Ps 19:7–14
INSTILLS TRUST	In the fear of the LORD one has strong confidence and his children have a refuge. **Proverbs 14:26**	Ps 25:14; Pr 18:10; Is 33:6
HOLDS MORE VALUE THAN GREAT TREASURE	Better a little with the fear of the LORD than great treasure with turmoil. **Proverbs 15:16**	Ps 37:16; Pr 16:8; Is 33:6; 1Tm 6:6
ENABLES US TO TURN FROM EVIL	Iniquity is atoned for by loyalty and faithfulness, and one turns from evil by the fear of the LORD. **Proverbs 16:6**	Ps 34:11–14; Pr 8:13

LEADS TO LIFE	The fear of the LORD leads to life; one will sleep at night without danger. **Proverbs 19:23**	Pr 10:27; 14:27; 19:23; 22:4
MOTIVATES US TO SHARE THE GOSPEL	Therefore, since we know the fear of the Lord, we try to persuade people. What we are is plain to God, and I hope it is also plain to your consciences. **2 Corinthians 5:11**	1Co 1:18–24; Jd 22–23
IS THE POSTURE OF GOD'S PEOPLE	Don't let your heart envy sinners; instead, always fear the LORD. **Proverbs 23:17**	Dt 10:12; Ec 12:13; Ac 9:31

FOR THE BATTLE IS HIS

Day 11

2 CHRONICLES 19:4–10

JEHOSHAPHAT'S REFORMS

⁴ Jehoshaphat lived in Jerusalem, and once again he went out among the people from Beer-sheba to the hill country of Ephraim and brought them back to the LORD, the God of their ancestors. ⁵ He appointed judges in all the fortified cities of the land of Judah, city by city. ⁶ Then he said to the judges, "Consider what you are doing, for you do not judge for a man, but for the LORD, who is with you in the matter of judgment. ⁷ And now, may the terror of the LORD be on you. Watch what you do, for there is no injustice or partiality or taking bribes with the LORD our God."

⁸ Jehoshaphat also appointed in Jerusalem some of the Levites and priests and some of the Israelite family heads for deciding the LORD's will and for settling disputes of the residents of Jerusalem. ⁹ He commanded them, saying, "In the fear of the LORD, with integrity, and wholeheartedly, you are to do the following: ¹⁰ For every dispute that comes to you from your brothers who dwell in their cities—whether it regards differences of bloodguilt, law, commandment, statutes, or judgments—you are to warn them, so they will not incur guilt before the LORD and wrath will not come on you and your brothers. Do this, and you will not incur guilt."

2 CHRONICLES 20:1–30

WAR AGAINST EASTERN ENEMIES

¹ After this, the Moabites and Ammonites, together with some of the Meunites, came to fight against Jehoshaphat. ² People came and told Jehoshaphat, "A vast number from beyond the Dead Sea and from Edom has come to fight against you; they are already in Hazazon-tamar" (that is, En-gedi). ³ Jehoshaphat was afraid, and he resolved to seek the LORD. Then he proclaimed a fast for all Judah, ⁴ who gathered to seek the LORD. They even came from all the cities of Judah to seek him.

JEHOSHAPHAT'S PRAYER

⁵ Then Jehoshaphat stood in the assembly of Judah and Jerusalem in the LORD's temple before the new courtyard. ⁶ He said:

LORD, God of our ancestors, are you not the God who is in heaven, and do you not rule over all the kingdoms of the nations? Power and might are in your hand, and no one can stand against you. ⁷ Are you not our God who drove out the inhabitants of this land before your people Israel and who gave it forever to the descendants of Abraham your friend? ⁸ They have lived in the land and have built you a sanctuary in it for your name and have said, [9] "If disaster comes on us—sword or judgment, pestilence or famine—we will stand before this temple and before you, for your name is in this temple. We will cry out to you because of our distress, and you will hear and deliver."

[10] Now here are the Ammonites, Moabites, and the inhabitants of Mount Seir. You did not let Israel invade them when Israel came out of the land of Egypt, but Israel turned away from them and did not destroy them. [11] Look how they repay us by coming to drive us out of your possession that you gave us as an inheritance. [12] Our God, will you not judge them? For we are powerless before this vast number that comes to fight against us. We do not know what to do, but we look to you.

GOD'S ANSWER

[13] All Judah was standing before the LORD with their dependents, their wives, and their children. [14] In the middle of the congregation, the Spirit of the LORD came on Jahaziel (son of Zechariah, son of Benaiah, son of Jeiel, son of Mattaniah, a Levite from Asaph's descendants), [15] and he said, "Listen carefully, all Judah and you inhabitants of Jerusalem, and King Jehoshaphat. This is what the LORD says: 'Do not be afraid or discouraged because of this vast number, for the battle is not yours, but God's. [16] Tomorrow, go down against them. You will see them coming up the Ascent of Ziz, and you will find them at the end of the valley facing the Wilderness of Jeruel. [17] You do not have to fight this battle.

Position yourselves, stand still, and see the salvation of the Lord.

He is with you, Judah and Jerusalem. Do not be afraid or discouraged. Tomorrow, go out to face them, for the LORD is with you.'"

[18] Then Jehoshaphat knelt low with his face to the ground, and all Judah and the inhabitants of Jerusalem fell down before the LORD to worship him. [19] Then the Levites from the sons of the Kohathites and the Korahites stood up to praise the LORD God of Israel shouting loudly.

VICTORY AND PLUNDER

[20] In the morning they got up early and went out to the wilderness of Tekoa. As they were about to go out, Jehoshaphat stood and said, "Hear me, Judah and you inhabitants of Jerusalem. Believe in the LORD your God, and you will be established; believe in his prophets, and you will succeed." [21] Then he consulted with the people and appointed some to sing for the LORD and some to praise the splendor of his holiness. When they went out in front of the armed forces, they kept singing:

Give thanks to the LORD,
for his faithful love endures forever.

[22] The moment they began their shouts and praises, the LORD set an ambush against the Ammonites, Moabites, and the inhabitants of Mount Seir who came to fight against Judah, and they were defeated. [23] The Ammonites and Moabites turned against the inhabitants of Mount Seir and completely annihilated them. When they had finished with the inhabitants of Seir, they helped destroy each other.

[24] When Judah came to a place overlooking the wilderness, they looked for the large army, but there were only corpses lying on the ground; nobody had escaped. [25] Then Jehoshaphat and his people went to gather the plunder. They found among them an abundance of goods on the bodies and valuable items. So they stripped them until nobody could carry any more. They were gathering the plunder for three days because there was so much. [26] They assembled in the Valley of Beracah on the fourth day, for there they blessed the LORD. Therefore, that place is still called the Valley of Beracah today.

[27] Then all the men of Judah and Jerusalem turned back with Jehoshaphat their leader, returning joyfully to Jerusalem, for the LORD enabled them to rejoice over their enemies. [28] So they came into Jerusalem to the LORD's temple with harps, lyres, and trumpets.

[29] The terror of God was on all the kingdoms of the lands when they heard that the LORD had fought against the enemies of Israel. [30] Then Jehoshaphat's kingdom was quiet, for his God gave him rest on every side.

PSALM 16

CONFIDENCE IN THE LORD

A Miktam of David.

[1] Protect me, God, for I take refuge in you.
[2] I said to the LORD, "You are my Lord;
I have nothing good besides you."
[3] As for the holy people who are in the land,
they are the noble ones.
All my delight is in them.
[4] The sorrows of those who take another god
for themselves will multiply;
I will not pour out their drink offerings of blood,
and I will not speak their names with my lips.

[5] LORD, you are my portion
and my cup of blessing;
you hold my future.
[6] The boundary lines have fallen for me
in pleasant places;
indeed, I have a beautiful inheritance.

[7] I will bless the LORD who counsels me—
even at night when my thoughts trouble me.
[8] I always let the LORD guide me.
Because he is at my right hand,
I will not be shaken.

[9] Therefore my heart is glad
and my whole being rejoices;
my body also rests securely.
[10] For you will not abandon me to Sheol;
you will not allow your faithful one to see decay.
[11] You reveal the path of life to me;
in your presence is abundant joy;
at your right hand are eternal pleasures.

1 THESSALONIANS 5:16–24

[16] Rejoice always, [17] pray constantly, [18] give thanks in everything; for this is God's will for you in Christ Jesus. [19] Don't stifle the Spirit. [20] Don't despise prophecies, [21] but test all things. Hold on to what is good. [22] Stay away from every kind of evil.

[23] Now may the God of peace himself sanctify you completely. And may your whole spirit, soul, and body be kept sound and blameless at the coming of our Lord Jesus Christ. [24] He who calls you is faithful; he will do it.

DAILY RESPONSE

What circumstances in 2 Chronicles 19 and 20 might
have led to fear?

What do these passages teach about God's character?

How do today's scriptures speak to similar circumstances
in your own life?

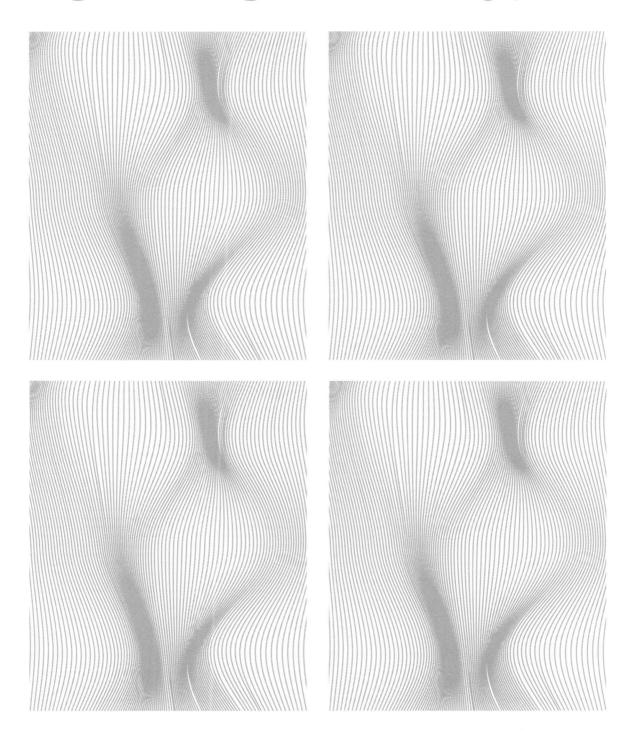

Day 12

ACTS 27:1–25

SAILING FOR ROME

¹ When it was decided that we were to sail to Italy, they handed over Paul and some other prisoners to a centurion named Julius, of the Imperial Regiment. ² When we had boarded a ship of Adramyttium, we put to sea, intending to sail to ports along the coast of Asia. Aristarchus, a Macedonian of Thessalonica, was with us. ³ The next day we put in at Sidon, and Julius treated Paul kindly and allowed him to go to his friends to receive their care. ⁴ When we had put out to sea from there, we sailed along the northern coast of Cyprus because the winds were against us. ⁵ After sailing through the open sea off Cilicia and Pamphylia, we reached Myra in Lycia. ⁶ There the centurion found an Alexandrian ship sailing for Italy and put us on board. ⁷ Sailing slowly for many days, with difficulty we arrived off Cnidus. Since the wind did not allow us to approach it, we sailed along the south side of Crete off Salmone. ⁸ With still more difficulty we sailed along the coast and came to a place called Fair Havens near the city of Lasea.

PAUL'S ADVICE IGNORED

⁹ By now much time had passed, and the voyage was already dangerous. Since the Day of Atonement was already over, Paul gave his advice ¹⁰ and told them, "Men, I can see that this voyage is headed toward disaster and heavy loss, not only of the cargo and the ship but also of our lives." ¹¹ But the centurion paid attention to the captain and the owner of the ship rather than to what Paul said. ¹² Since the harbor was unsuitable to winter in, the majority decided to set sail from there, hoping somehow to reach Phoenix, a harbor on Crete facing the southwest and northwest, and to winter there.

STORM-TOSSED SHIP

¹³ When a gentle south wind sprang up, they thought they had achieved their purpose. They weighed anchor and sailed along the shore of Crete. ¹⁴ But before long, a fierce wind called the "northeaster" rushed down from the island. ¹⁵ Since the ship was caught and unable to head into the wind, we gave way to it and were driven along. ¹⁶ After running under the shelter of a little island called Cauda, we were barely able to get control of the skiff. ¹⁷ After hoisting it up, they used ropes and tackle and girded the ship. Fearing they would run aground on the Syrtis, they lowered the drift-anchor, and in this way they were driven along. ¹⁸ Because we were being severely battered by the storm, they began to jettison the cargo the next day. ¹⁹ On the third day, they threw the ship's tackle overboard with their own hands. ²⁰ For many days neither sun nor stars appeared, and the severe storm kept raging. Finally all hope was fading that we would be saved.

²¹ Since they had been without food for a long time, Paul then stood up among them and said, "You men should have followed my advice not to sail from Crete and sustain this damage and loss. ²² Now I urge you to take courage, because there will be no loss of any of your lives, but only of the ship. ²³ For last night an angel of the God I belong to and serve stood by me ²⁴ and said, 'Don't be afraid, Paul. It is necessary for you to appear before Caesar. And indeed, God has graciously given you all those who are sailing with you.' ²⁵ So take courage, men, because I believe God that it will be just the way it was told to me."

PSALM 37:16–19

¹⁶ The little that the righteous person has is better
than the abundance of many wicked people.
¹⁷ For the arms of the wicked will be broken,
but the Lord supports the righteous.

¹⁸ The Lord watches over the blameless all their days,
and their inheritance will last forever.
¹⁹ They will not be disgraced in times of adversity;
they will be satisfied in days of hunger.

JEREMIAH 17:7–8

[7] "The person who trusts in the LORD,
whose confidence indeed is the LORD, is blessed.

[8] He will be like a tree planted by water:
it sends its roots out toward a stream,
it doesn't fear when heat comes,
and its foliage remains green.
It will not worry in a year of drought
or cease producing fruit."

2 CORINTHIANS 4:7–10

TREASURE IN CLAY JARS

[7] Now we have this treasure in clay jars, so that this extraordinary power may be from God and not from us. [8] We are afflicted in every way but not crushed; we are perplexed but not in despair; [9] we are persecuted but not abandoned; we are struck down but not destroyed. [10] We always carry the death of Jesus in our body, so that the life of Jesus may also be displayed in our body.

DAILY RESPONSE

What circumstances in Acts 27 might have led to fear?

What does this passage teach about God's character?

How do today's scriptures speak to similar circumstances
in your own life?

IT IS WELL

WITH MY SOUL

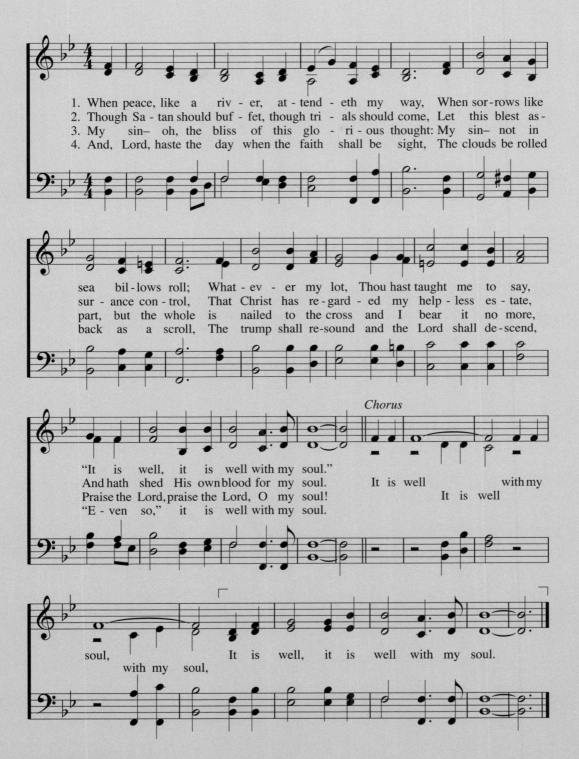

1. When peace, like a riv - er, at - tend - eth my way, When sor-rows like
2. Though Sa - tan should buf - fet, though tri - als should come, Let this blest as -
3. My sin— oh, the bliss of this glo - ri - ous thought: My sin— not in
4. And, Lord, haste the day when the faith shall be sight, The clouds be rolled

sea bil-lows roll; What - ev - er my lot, Thou hast taught me to say,
sur - ance con - trol, That Christ has re-gard - ed my help - less es - tate,
part, but the whole is nailed to the cross and I bear it no more,
back as a scroll, The trump shall re-sound and the Lord shall de-scend,

Chorus

"It is well, it is well with my soul."
And hath shed His own blood for my soul.
Praise the Lord, praise the Lord, O my soul!
"E - ven so," it is well with my soul.

It is well with my
It is well

soul, It is well, it is well with my soul.
with my soul,

WORDS: Horatio G. Spafford
MUSIC: Philip P. Bliss

GRACE

DAY

Take this day to catch up on your reading,
pray, and rest in the presence of the Lord.

13

The LORD is my light and my salvation— whom should I fear? The LORD is the stronghold of my life— whom should I dread?

PSALM 27:1

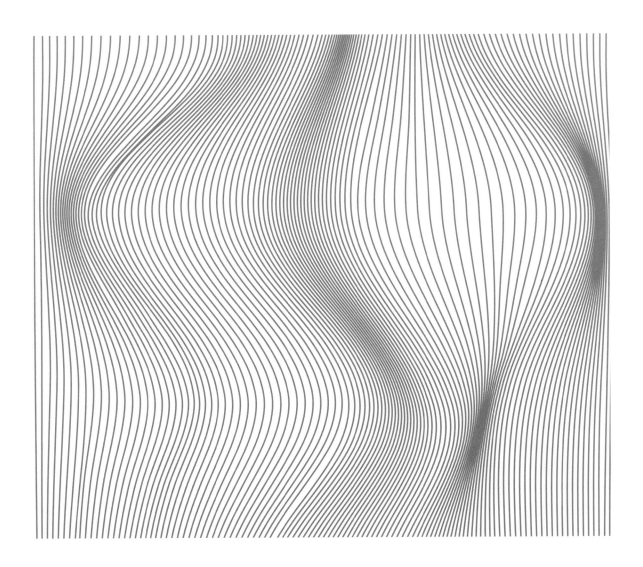

WEEKLY TRUTH   Day 14

Scripture is God-breathed and true. When we memorize it, we carry the good news of Jesus with us wherever we go.

This week, we will continue memorizing Isaiah 43:1–2 by adding the second verse. God has promised He will be with us in every circumstance, no matter how difficult or trying.

Now this is what the LORD says—the one who created you, Jacob, and the one who formed you, Israel—"Do not fear, for I have redeemed you; I have called you by your name; you are mine. When you pass through the waters, I will be with you, and the rivers will not overwhelm you. When you walk through the fire, you will not be scorched, and the flame will not burn you."

ISAIAH 43:1–2

See tips for memorizing Scripture on page 108!

FOR HE WILL NOT LEAVE YOU

Day 15

JOSHUA 1:1–18

ENCOURAGEMENT OF JOSHUA

[1] After the death of Moses the LORD's servant, the LORD spoke to Joshua son of Nun, Moses's assistant: [2] "Moses my servant is dead. Now you and all the people prepare to cross over the Jordan to the land I am giving the Israelites. [3] I have given you every place where the sole of your foot treads, just as I promised Moses. [4] Your territory will be from the wilderness and Lebanon to the great river, the Euphrates River—all the land of the Hittites—and west to the Mediterranean Sea. [5] No one will be able to stand against you as long as you live. I will be with you, just as I was with Moses. I will not leave you or abandon you.

[6] "Be strong and courageous, for you will distribute the land I swore to their ancestors to give them as an inheritance. [7] Above all, be strong and very courageous to observe carefully the whole instruction my servant Moses commanded you. Do not turn from it to the right or the left, so that you will have success wherever you go. [8] This book of instruction must not depart from your mouth; you are to meditate on it day and night so that you may carefully observe everything written in it. For then you will prosper and succeed in whatever you do. [9] Haven't I commanded you: be strong and courageous? Do not be afraid or discouraged, for the LORD your God is with you wherever you go."

JOSHUA PREPARES THE PEOPLE

[10] Then Joshua commanded the officers of the people, [11] "Go through the camp and tell the people, 'Get provisions ready for yourselves, for within three days you will be crossing the Jordan to go in and take possession of the land the LORD your God is giving you to inherit.'"

[12] Joshua said to the Reubenites, the Gadites, and half the tribe of Manasseh, [13] "Remember what Moses the LORD's servant commanded you when he said, 'The LORD your God will give you rest, and he will give you this land.' [14] Your wives, dependents, and livestock may remain in the land Moses gave you on this side of the Jordan. But your best soldiers must cross over in battle formation ahead of your brothers and help them [15] until the LORD gives your brothers rest, as he has given you, and they too possess the land the LORD your God is giving them. You may then return to the land of your inheritance and take possession of what Moses the LORD's servant gave you on the east side of the Jordan."

[16] They answered Joshua, "Everything you have commanded us we will do, and everywhere you send us we will go. [17] We will obey you, just as we obeyed Moses in everything. Certainly the LORD your God will be with you, as he was with Moses. [18] Anyone who rebels against your order and does not obey your words in all that you command him, will be put to death. Above all, be strong and courageous!"

PSALM 91

THE PROTECTION OF THE MOST HIGH

[1] The one who lives under the protection of the Most High dwells in the shadow of the Almighty.

[2] I will say concerning the LORD, who is my refuge and
  my fortress,
my God in whom I trust:
[3] He himself will rescue you from the bird trap,
from the destructive plague.

[4] **He will cover you with
  his feathers;
you will take refuge under
  his wings.
His faithfulness will be
  a protective shield.**

[5] You will not fear the terror of the night,
the arrow that flies by day,
[6] the plague that stalks in darkness,
or the pestilence that ravages at noon.
[7] Though a thousand fall at your side
and ten thousand at your right hand,
the pestilence will not reach you.
[8] You will only see it with your eyes
and witness the punishment of the wicked.

[9] Because you have made the LORD—my refuge,
the Most High—your dwelling place,
[10] no harm will come to you;
no plague will come near your tent.
[11] For he will give his angels orders concerning you,
to protect you in all your ways.
[12] They will support you with their hands
so that you will not strike your foot against a stone.
[13] You will tread on the lion and the cobra;
you will trample the young lion and the serpent.

[14] Because he has his heart set on me,
I will deliver him;
I will protect him because he knows my name.
[15] When he calls out to me, I will answer him;
I will be with him in trouble.
I will rescue him and give him honor.
[16] I will satisfy him with a long life
and show him my salvation.

JOHN 14:25–27

[25] "I have spoken these things to you while I remain with you. [26] But the Counselor, the Holy Spirit, whom the Father will send in my name, will teach you all things and remind you of everything I have told you.

[27] "Peace I leave with you. My peace I give to you. I do not give to you as the world gives. Don't let your heart be troubled or fearful."

DAILY RESPONSE

What circumstances in Joshua 1 might have led to fear?

What does this passage teach about God's character?

How do today's scriptures speak to similar circumstances
in your own life?

FOR HE RESCUES AND DELIVERS

Day 16

DANIEL 6

THE PLOT AGAINST DANIEL

[1] Darius decided to appoint 120 satraps over the kingdom, stationed throughout the realm, [2] and over them three administrators, including Daniel. These satraps would be accountable to them so that the king would not be defrauded. [3] Daniel distinguished himself above the administrators and satraps because he had an extraordinary spirit, so the king planned to set him over the whole realm. [4] The administrators and satraps, therefore, kept trying to find a charge against Daniel regarding the kingdom. But they could find no charge or corruption, for he was trustworthy, and no negligence or corruption was found in him. [5] Then these men said, "We will never find any charge against this Daniel unless we find something against him concerning the law of his God."

[6] So the administrators and satraps went together to the king and said to him, "May King Darius live forever. [7] All the administrators of the kingdom—the prefects, satraps, advisers, and governors—have agreed that the king should establish an ordinance and enforce an edict that, for thirty days, anyone who petitions any god or man except you, the king, will be thrown into the lions' den. [8] Therefore, Your Majesty, establish the edict and sign the document so that, as a law of the Medes and Persians, it is irrevocable and cannot be changed." [9] So King Darius signed the written edict.

DANIEL IN THE LIONS' DEN

[10] When Daniel learned that the document had been signed, he went into his house. The windows in its upstairs room opened toward Jerusalem, and three times a day he got down on his knees, prayed, and gave thanks to his God, just as he had done before. [11] Then these men went as a group and found Daniel petitioning and imploring his God. [12] So they approached the king and asked about his edict: "Didn't you sign an edict that for thirty days any person who petitions any god or man except you, the king, will be thrown into the lions' den?"

The king answered, "As a law of the Medes and Persians, the order stands and is irrevocable."

¹³ Then they replied to the king, "Daniel, one of the Judean exiles, has ignored you, the king, and the edict you signed, for he prays three times a day." ¹⁴ As soon as the king heard this, he was very displeased; he set his mind on rescuing Daniel and made every effort until sundown to deliver him.

¹⁵ Then these men went together to the king and said to him, "You know, Your Majesty, that it is a law of the Medes and Persians that no edict or ordinance the king establishes can be changed."

¹⁶ So the king gave the order, and they brought Daniel and threw him into the lions' den. The king said to Daniel,

"May your God, whom you continually serve, rescue you!"

¹⁷ A stone was brought and placed over the mouth of the den. The king sealed it with his own signet ring and with the signet rings of his nobles, so that nothing in regard to Daniel could be changed. ¹⁸ Then the king went to his palace and spent the night fasting. No diversions were brought to him, and he could not sleep.

DANIEL RELEASED

¹⁹ At the first light of dawn the king got up and hurried to the lions' den. ²⁰ When he reached the den, he cried out in anguish to Daniel. "Daniel, servant of the living God," the king said, "has your God, whom you continually serve, been able to rescue you from the lions?"

²¹ Then Daniel spoke with the king: "May the king live forever. ²² My God sent his angel and shut the lions' mouths; and they haven't harmed me, for I was found innocent before him. And also before you, Your Majesty, I have not done harm."

²³ The king was overjoyed and gave orders to take Daniel out of the den. When Daniel was brought up from the den, he was found to be unharmed, for he trusted in his God. ²⁴ The king then gave the command, and those men who had maliciously accused Daniel were brought and thrown into the lions' den—they, their children, and their wives. They had not reached the bottom of the den before the lions overpowered them and crushed all their bones.

DARIUS HONORS GOD

²⁵ Then King Darius wrote to those of every people, nation, and language who live on the whole earth: "May your prosperity abound. ²⁶ I issue a decree that in all my royal dominion, people must tremble in fear before the God of Daniel:

> For he is the living God,
> and he endures forever;
> his kingdom will never be destroyed,
> and his dominion has no end.
> ²⁷ He rescues and delivers;
> he performs signs and wonders
> in the heavens and on the earth,
> for he has rescued Daniel
> from the power of the lions."

²⁸ So Daniel prospered during the reign of Darius and the reign of Cyrus the Persian.

PSALM 37:1–11

INSTRUCTION IN WISDOM

Of David.

¹ Do not be agitated by evildoers;
do not envy those who do wrong.
² For they wither quickly like grass
and wilt like tender green plants.

³ Trust in the Lᴏʀᴅ and do what is good;
dwell in the land and live securely.
⁴ Take delight in the Lᴏʀᴅ,
and he will give you your heart's desires.

⁵ Commit your way to the Lᴏʀᴅ;
trust in him, and he will act,
⁶ making your righteousness shine like the dawn,
your justice like the noonday.

⁷ Be silent before the Lᴏʀᴅ and wait expectantly for him;

do not be agitated by one who prospers in his way,
by the person who carries out evil plans.

[8] Refrain from anger and give up your rage;
do not be agitated—it can only bring harm.
[9] For evildoers will be destroyed,
but those who put their hope in the LORD
will inherit the land.

[10] A little while, and the wicked person will be no more;
though you look for him, he will not be there.
[11] But the humble will inherit the land
and will enjoy abundant prosperity.

ISAIAH 26:3–4

[3] You will keep the mind that is dependent on you
in perfect peace,
for it is trusting in you.
[4] Trust in the LORD forever,
because in the LORD, the LORD himself, is an everlasting rock!

JAMES 1:2–5

TRIALS AND MATURITY

[2] Consider it a great joy, my brothers and sisters, whenever you experience various trials, [3] because you know that the testing of your faith produces endurance. [4] And let endurance have its full effect, so that you may be mature and complete, lacking nothing.

[5] Now if any of you lacks wisdom, he should ask God—who gives to all generously and ungrudgingly—and it will be given to him.

DAILY RESPONSE

What circumstances in Daniel 6 might have led to fear?

What does this passage teach about God's character?

How do today's scriptures speak to similar circumstances
in your own life?

FOR HE IS YOUR PEACE

Day 17

JUDGES 6:1–24

MIDIAN OPPRESSES ISRAEL

¹ The Israelites did what was evil in the sight of the Lord. So the Lord handed them over to Midian seven years, ² and they oppressed Israel. Because of Midian, the Israelites made hiding places for themselves in the mountains, caves, and strongholds. ³ Whenever the Israelites planted crops, the Midianites, Amalekites, and the people of the east came and attacked them. ⁴ They encamped against them and destroyed the produce of the land, even as far as Gaza. They left nothing for Israel to eat, as well as no sheep, ox, or donkey. ⁵ For the Midianites came with their cattle and their tents like a great swarm of locusts. They and their camels were without number, and they entered the land to lay waste to it. ⁶ So Israel became poverty-stricken because of Midian, and the Israelites cried out to the Lord.

⁷ When the Israelites cried out to him because of Midian, ⁸ the Lord sent a prophet to them. He said to them, "This is what the Lord God of Israel says: 'I brought you out of Egypt and out of the place of slavery. ⁹ I rescued you from the power of Egypt and the power of all who oppressed you. I drove them out before you and gave you their land. ¹⁰ I said to you: I am the Lord your God. Do not fear the gods of the Amorites whose land you live in. But you did not obey me.'"

THE LORD CALLS GIDEON

¹¹ The angel of the Lord came, and he sat under the oak that was in Ophrah, which belonged to Joash, the Abiezrite. His son Gideon was threshing wheat in the winepress in order to hide it from the Midianites. ¹² Then the angel of the Lord appeared to him and said, "The Lord is with you, valiant warrior."

¹³ Gideon said to him, "Please, my lord, if the Lord is with us, why has all this happened? And where are all his wonders that our ancestors told us about? They said, 'Hasn't the Lord brought us out of Egypt?' But now the Lord has abandoned us and handed us over to Midian."

¹⁴ The Lord turned to him and said, "Go in the strength you have and deliver Israel from the grasp of Midian. I am sending you!"

¹⁵ He said to him, "Please, Lord, how can I deliver Israel? Look, my family is the weakest in Manasseh, and I am the youngest in my father's family."

¹⁶ "But I will be with you," the Lord said to him. "You will strike Midian down as if it were one man."

¹⁷ Then he said to him, "If I have found favor with you, give me a sign that you are speaking with me. ¹⁸ Please do not leave this place until I return to you. Let me bring my gift and set it before you."

And he said, "I will stay until you return."

¹⁹ So Gideon went and prepared a young goat and unleavened bread from a half bushel of flour. He placed the meat in a basket and the broth in a pot. He brought them out and offered them to him under the oak.

²⁰ The angel of God said to him, "Take the meat with the unleavened bread, put it on this stone, and pour the broth on it." So he did that.

²¹ The angel of the Lord extended the tip of the staff that was in his hand and touched the meat and the unleavened bread. Fire came up from the rock and consumed the meat and the unleavened bread. Then the angel of the Lord vanished from his sight.

²² When Gideon realized that he was the angel of the Lord, he said, "Oh no, Lord God! I have seen the angel of the Lord face to face!"

²³ But the Lord said to him, "Peace to you. Don't be afraid, for you will not die." ²⁴ So Gideon built an altar to the Lord

there and called it The Lord Is Peace. It is still in Ophrah of the Abiezrites today.

PSALM 23

THE GOOD SHEPHERD

A psalm of David.

¹ The Lord is my shepherd;
I have what I need.
² He lets me lie down in green pastures;
he leads me beside quiet waters.

³ **He renews my life;**
he leads me along the right paths
for his name's sake.

⁴ Even when I go through the darkest valley,
I fear no danger,
for you are with me;
your rod and your staff—they comfort me.

⁵ You prepare a table before me
in the presence of my enemies;
you anoint my head with oil;
my cup overflows.
⁶ Only goodness and faithful love will pursue me
all the days of my life,
and I will dwell in the house of the Lord
as long as I live.

ISAIAH 30:18

Therefore the Lord is waiting to show you mercy,
and is rising up to show you compassion,
for the Lord is a just God.
All who wait patiently for him are happy.

2 TIMOTHY 2:13

...if we are faithless, he remains faithful,
for he cannot deny himself.

DAILY RESPONSE

What circumstances in Judges 6 might have led to fear?

What does this passage teach about God's character?

How do today's scriptures speak to similar circumstances
in your own life?

ST. PATRICK'S BREASTPLATE

Christ be with me, Christ within me,

Christ behind me, Christ before me,

Christ beside me, Christ to win me,

Christ to comfort and restore me,

Christ beneath me, Christ above me,

Christ in quiet, Christ in danger,

Christ in hearts of all that love me,

Christ in mouth of friend and stranger.

DO NOT FEAR

FOR HE SENDS YOU

Day 18

EXODUS 3:1–14

MOSES AND THE BURNING BUSH

¹ Meanwhile, Moses was shepherding the flock of his father-in-law Jethro, the priest of Midian. He led the flock to the far side of the wilderness and came to Horeb, the mountain of God. ² Then the angel of the LORD appeared to him in a flame of fire within a bush. As Moses looked, he saw that the bush was on fire but was not consumed. ³ So Moses thought, "I must go over and look at this remarkable sight. Why isn't the bush burning up?"

⁴ When the LORD saw that he had gone over to look, God called out to him from the bush, "Moses, Moses!"

"Here I am," he answered.

⁵ "Do not come closer," he said. "Remove the sandals from your feet, for the place where you are standing is holy ground." ⁶ Then he continued, "I am the God of your father, the God of Abraham, the God of Isaac, and the God of Jacob." Moses hid his face because he was afraid to look at God.

⁷ Then the LORD said, "I have observed the misery of my people in Egypt, and have heard them crying out because of their oppressors. I know about their sufferings, ⁸ and I have come down to rescue them from the power of the Egyptians and to bring them from that land to a good and spacious land, a land flowing with milk and honey—the territory of the Canaanites, Hethites, Amorites, Perizzites, Hivites, and Jebusites. ⁹ So because the Israelites' cry for help has come to me, and I have also seen the way the Egyptians are oppressing

them, ¹⁰ therefore, go. I am sending you to Pharaoh so that you may lead my people, the Israelites, out of Egypt."

¹¹ But Moses asked God, "Who am I that I should go to Pharaoh and that I should bring the Israelites out of Egypt?"

¹² He answered, "I will certainly be with you, and this will be the sign to you that I am the one who sent you: when you bring the people out of Egypt, you will all worship God at this mountain."

¹³ Then Moses asked God, "If I go to the Israelites and say to them, 'The God of your ancestors has sent me to you,' and they ask me, 'What is his name?' what should I tell them?"

¹⁴ God replied to Moses, "I AM WHO I AM. This is what you are to say to the Israelites: I AM has sent me to you."

PSALM 46:1–7

GOD OUR REFUGE

For the choir director. A song of the sons of Korah. According to Alamoth.

¹ God is our refuge and strength,
a helper who is always found
in times of trouble.
² Therefore we will not be afraid,
though the earth trembles

and the mountains topple
into the depths of the seas,
³ though its water roars and foams
and the mountains quake with its turmoil.   *Selah*

⁴ There is a river—
its streams delight the city of God,
the holy dwelling place of the Most High.
⁵ God is within her; she will not be toppled.
God will help her when the morning dawns.
⁶ Nations rage, kingdoms topple;
the earth melts when he lifts his voice.
⁷ The LORD of Armies is with us;
the God of Jacob is our stronghold.   *Selah*

LUKE 12:11–12

¹¹ "Whenever they bring you before synagogues and rulers and authorities, don't worry about how you should defend yourselves or what you should say. ¹² For the Holy Spirit will teach you at that very hour what must be said."

1 PETER 5:6–11

⁶ Humble yourselves, therefore, under the mighty hand of God, so that he may exalt you at the proper time, ⁷ casting all your cares on him, because he cares about you. ⁸ Be sober-minded, be alert. Your adversary the devil is prowling around like a roaring lion, looking for anyone he can devour. ⁹ Resist him, firm in the faith, knowing that the same kind of sufferings are being experienced by your fellow believers throughout the world.

¹⁰ The God of all grace, who called you to his eternal glory in Christ, will himself restore, establish, strengthen, and support you after you have suffered a little while. ¹¹ To him be dominion forever. Amen.

DAILY RESPONSE

What circumstances in Exodus 3 might have led to fear?

What does this passage teach about God's character?

How do today's scriptures speak to similar circumstances
in your own life?

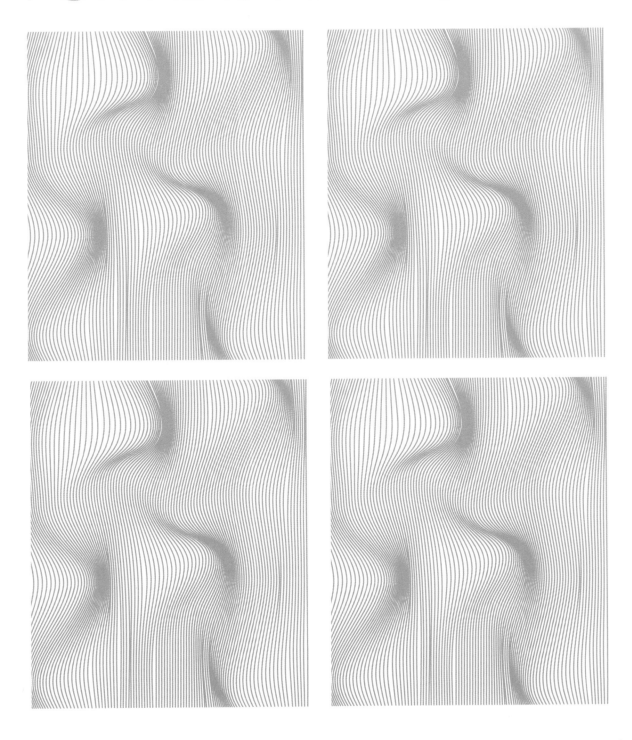

MARK 5:21–43

A GIRL RESTORED AND A WOMAN HEALED

[21] When Jesus had crossed over again by boat to the other side, a large crowd gathered around him while he was by the sea. [22] One of the synagogue leaders, named Jairus, came, and when he saw Jesus, he fell at his feet [23] and begged him earnestly, "My little daughter is dying. Come and lay your hands on her so that she can get well and live." [24] So Jesus went with him, and a large crowd was following and pressing against him.

[25] Now a woman suffering from bleeding for twelve years [26] had endured much under many doctors. She had spent everything she had and was not helped at all. On the contrary, she became worse. [27] Having heard about Jesus, she came up behind him in the crowd and touched his clothing. [28] For she said, "If I just touch his clothes, I'll be made well." [29] Instantly her flow of blood ceased, and she sensed in her body that she was healed of her affliction.

[30] Immediately Jesus realized that power had gone out from him. He turned around in the crowd and said, "Who touched my clothes?"

[31] His disciples said to him, "You see the crowd pressing against you, and yet you say, 'Who touched me?'"

[32] But he was looking around to see who had done this. [33] The woman, with fear and trembling, knowing what had happened to her, came and fell down before him, and told him the whole truth. [34] "Daughter," he said to her, "your faith has saved you. Go in peace and be healed from your affliction."

[35] While he was still speaking, people came from the synagogue leader's house and said, "Your daughter is dead. Why bother the teacher anymore?"

[36] When Jesus overheard what was said, he told the synagogue leader, "Don't be afraid. Only believe." [37] He did not let anyone accompany him except Peter, James, and John, James's brother. [38] They came to the leader's house, and he saw a commotion—people weeping and wailing loudly. [39] He went in and said to them, "Why are you making a commotion and weeping? The child is not dead but asleep." [40] They laughed at him, but he put them all outside. He took the child's father, mother, and those who were with him, and entered the place where the child was. [41] Then he took the child by the hand and said to her, "Talitha koum" (which is translated, "Little girl, I say to you, get up"). [42] Immediately the girl got up and began to walk. (She was twelve years old.) At this they were utterly astounded. [43] Then he gave them strict orders that no one should know about this and told them to give her something to eat.

PROVERBS 4:20–22

THE STRAIGHT PATH

[20] My son, pay attention to my words;
listen closely to my sayings.
[21] Don't lose sight of them;
keep them within your heart.
[22] For they are life to those who find them,
and health to one's whole body.

2 CORINTHIANS 4:17–18

[17] For our momentary light affliction is producing for us an absolutely incomparable eternal weight of glory. [18] So we do not focus on what is seen, but on what is unseen. For what is seen is temporary, but what is unseen is eternal.

REVELATION 21:1–6

THE NEW CREATION

¹ Then I saw a new heaven and a new earth; for the first heaven and the first earth had passed away, and the sea was no more. ² I also saw the holy city, the new Jerusalem, coming down out of heaven from God, prepared like a bride adorned for her husband.

³ Then I heard a loud voice from the throne: Look, God's dwelling is with humanity, and he will live with them. They will be his peoples, and God himself will be with them and will be their God. ⁴ He will wipe away every tear from their eyes. Death will be no more; grief, crying, and pain will be no more, because the previous things have passed away.

⁵ Then the one seated on the throne said, "Look, I am making everything new." He also said, "Write, because these words are faithful and true." ⁶ Then he said to me, "It is done! I am the Alpha and the Omega, the beginning and the end. I will freely give to the thirsty from the spring of the water of life."

DAILY RESPONSE

What circumstances in Mark 5 might have led to fear?

What does this passage teach about God's character?

How do today's scriptures speak to similar circumstances
in your own life?

GRACE

DAY

Take this day to catch up on your reading,
pray, and rest in the presence of the Lord.

20

God is our refuge and strength, a helper who is always found in times of trouble.

PSALM 46:1

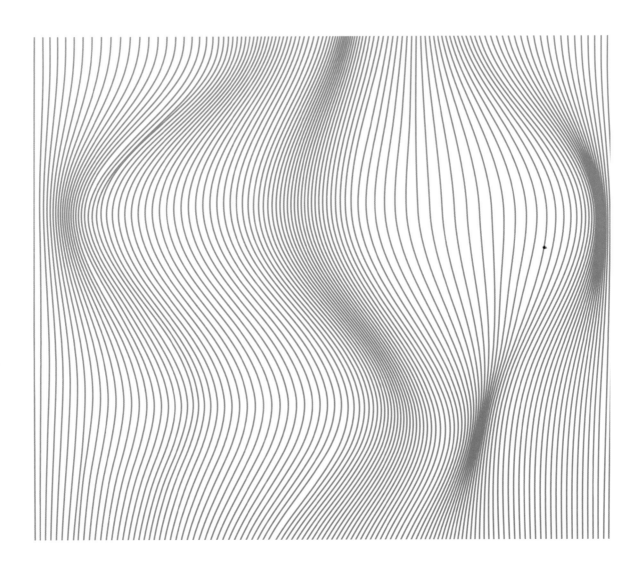

WEEKLY TRUTH   **Day 21**

Scripture is God-breathed and true. When we memorize it, we carry the good news of Jesus with us wherever we go.

Over the course of this reading plan, we have memorized Isaiah 43:1–2. Spend some time reviewing the entire passage to strengthen your memorization, reminding yourself that God's presence and promises hold in every circumstance you may face.

Now this is what the LORD says—the one who created you, Jacob, and the one who formed you, Israel—"Do not fear, for I have redeemed you; I have called you by your name; you are mine. When you pass through the waters, I will be with you, and the rivers will not overwhelm you. When you walk through the fire, you will not be scorched, and the flame will not burn you."

ISAIAH 43:1–2

See tips for memorizing Scripture on page 108!

FINAL REFLECTION

Think back on your time in Scripture over the last three weeks. How does God's faithful presence equip you to respond to fear differently?

Which Scripture or days felt most relevant to the fears you listed on page 18 at the beginning of this study?

What did Scripture reveal about the roots of your fears?

Knowing times of fear are still to come, what did you learn about God in this study that you can hold on to moving forward?

What practices or habits from pages 33–35 do you want to continue to cultivate as reminders of God's constant presence in your life? How could an increased sense of His presence be a comfort to you in times of fear?

BENEDICTION

And what more can I say? Time is too short for me to tell about Gideon, Barak, Samson, Jephthah, David, Samuel, and the prophets, who by faith conquered kingdoms, administered justice, obtained promises, shut the mouths of lions, quenched the raging of fire, escaped the edge of the sword, gained strength in weakness, became mighty in battle, and put foreign armies to flight. Women received their dead, raised to life again. Other people were tortured, not accepting release, so that they might gain a better resurrection. Others experienced mockings and scourgings, as well as bonds and imprisonment. They were stoned, they were sawed in two, they died by the sword, they wandered about in sheepskins, in goatskins, destitute, afflicted, and mistreated. The world was not worthy of them. They wandered in deserts and on mountains, hiding in caves and holes in the ground. All these were approved through their faith, but they did not receive what was promised, since God had provided something better for us, so that they would not be made perfect without us.

HEBREWS 11:32–40

"You will have suffering in this world.
Be courageous! I have conquered the world."

JOHN 16:33

Tips for Memorizing Scripture

At She Reads Truth, we believe Scripture memorization is an important discipline in your walk with God. Committing God's Truth to memory means He can minister to us—and we can minister to others—through His Word no matter where we are. As you approach the Weekly Truth passage in this book, try these memorization tips to see which techniques work best for you!

STUDY IT

Study the passage in its biblical context and ask yourself a few questions before you begin to memorize it: What does this passage say? What does it mean? How would I say this in my own words? What does it teach me about God? Understanding what the passage means helps you know why it is important to carry it with you wherever you go.

Break the passage into smaller sections, memorizing a phrase at a time.

PRAY IT

Use the passage you are memorizing as a prompt for prayer.

WRITE IT

Dedicate a notebook to Scripture memorization and write the passage over and over again.

Diagram the passage after you write it out. Place a square around the verbs, underline the nouns, and circle any adjectives or adverbs. Say the passage aloud several times, emphasizing the verbs as you repeat it. Then do the same thing again with the nouns, then the adjectives and adverbs.

Write out the first letter of each word in the passage somewhere you can reference it throughout the week as you work on your memorization.

Use a whiteboard to write out the passage. Erase a few words at a time as you continue to repeat it aloud. Keep erasing parts of the passage until you have it all committed to memory.

CREATE

If you can, make up a tune for the passage to sing as you go about your day, or try singing it to the tune of a favorite song.

Sketch the passage, visualizing what each phrase would look like in the form of a picture. Or, try using calligraphy or altering the style of your handwriting as you write it out.

Use hand signals or signs to come up with associations for each word or phrase and repeat the movements as you practice.

SAY IT

Repeat the passage out loud to yourself as you are going through the rhythm of your day—getting ready, pouring your coffee, waiting in traffic, or making dinner.

Listen to the passage read aloud to you.

Record a voice memo on your phone and listen to it throughout the day or play it on an audio Bible.

SHARE IT

Memorize the passage with a friend, family member, or mentor. Spontaneously challenge each other to recite the passage, or pick a time to review your passage and practice saying it from memory together.

Send the passage as an encouraging text to a friend, testing yourself as you type to see how much you have memorized so far.

KEEP AT IT!

Set reminders on your phone to prompt you to practice your passage.

Purchase a She Reads Truth 12 Card Set or keep a stack of notecards with Scripture you are memorizing by your bed. Practice reciting what you've memorized previously before you go to sleep, ending with the passages you are currently learning. If you wake up in the middle of the night, review them again instead of grabbing your phone. Read them out loud before you get out of bed in the morning.

Download the free Weekly Truth lock screens for your phone on the She Reads Truth app and read the passage throughout the day when you check your phone.

CSB BOOK ABBREVIATIONS

OLD TESTAMENT

GN Genesis	**JB** Job	**HAB** Habakkuk	**PHP** Philippians
EX Exodus	**PS** Psalms	**ZPH** Zephaniah	**COL** Colossians
LV Leviticus	**PR** Proverbs	**HG** Haggai	**1TH** 1 Thessalonians
NM Numbers	**EC** Ecclesiastes	**ZCH** Zechariah	**2TH** 2 Thessalonians
DT Deuteronomy	**SG** Song of Solomon	**MAL** Malachi	**1TM** 1 Timothy
JOS Joshua	**IS** Isaiah		**2TM** 2 Timothy
JDG Judges	**JR** Jeremiah		**TI** Titus
RU Ruth	**LM** Lamentations	### NEW TESTAMENT	**PHM** Philemon
1SM 1 Samuel	**EZK** Ezekiel	**MT** Matthew	**HEB** Hebrews
2SM 2 Samuel	**DN** Daniel	**MK** Mark	**JMS** James
1KG 1 Kings	**HS** Hosea	**LK** Luke	**1PT** 1 Peter
2KG 2 Kings	**JL** Joel	**JN** John	**2PT** 2 Peter
1CH 1 Chronicles	**AM** Amos	**AC** Acts	**1JN** 1 John
2CH 2 Chronicles	**OB** Obadiah	**RM** Romans	**2JN** 2 John
EZR Ezra	**JNH** Jonah	**1CO** 1 Corinthians	**3JN** 3 John
NEH Nehemiah	**MC** Micah	**2CO** 2 Corinthians	**JD** Jude
EST Esther	**NAH** Nahum	**GL** Galatians	**RV** Revelation
		EPH Ephesians	

BIBLIOGRAPHY

The New Encyclopedia of Christian Quotations. Compiled by Mark Water. Grand Rapids: Baker Books, 2000.

LOOKING FOR DEVOTIONALS?

Download the **She Reads Truth app** to find devotionals that complement your daily Scripture reading. If you're stuck on a passage, hop into the community discussion to instantly connect with other Shes who are reading God's Word right along with you. You can also highlight Bible passages and download free lock screens for Weekly Truth memorization—all on the She Reads Truth app.

DOWNLOAD THE
SHE READS TRUTH
APP TODAY!

You just spent 21 days in the Word of God!

**MY FAVORITE DAY OF
THIS READING PLAN:**

**ONE THING I LEARNED
ABOUT GOD:**

**WHAT WAS GOD DOING IN
MY LIFE DURING THIS STUDY?**

HOW DID I FIND DELIGHT IN GOD'S WORD?

**WHAT DID I LEARN THAT I WANT TO SHARE
WITH SOMEONE ELSE?**

**A SPECIFIC SCRIPTURE THAT
ENCOURAGED ME:**

**A SPECIFIC SCRIPTURE THAT
CHALLENGED AND CONVICTED ME:**